The Constitution of the
State of Delaware:
A Quick Reference Guide

Bootblack Budget Books
Copyright 2018 ©
ISBN-13: 978-1985832497
ISBN-10: 1985832496

Contents:

PREAMBLE – Page 26

ARTICLE I: BILL OF RIGHTS – Page 27

Section 1. Freedom of religion.

Section 2. Religious test for office not required.

Section 3. Free and equal elections.

Section 4. Trial by jury.

Section 5. Freedom of press and speech; evidence in libel prosecutions; jury questions.

Section 6. Searches and seizures.

Section 7. Procedural rights in criminal prosecutions; jury trial; self-incrimination; deprivation of life, liberty or property.

Section 8. Prosecution by indictment or information; double jeopardy; just compensation for property.

Section 9. Courts shall be open; remedy for injury; suits against State.

Section 10. Suspension of laws by General Assembly.

Section 11. Excessive bail or fines; cruel punishments; health of prisoners.

Section 12. Right to bail; access to accused.

Section 13. Suspension of habeas corpus.

Section 14. Commission of oyer and terminer, or jail delivery.

Section 15. Corruption of blood; forfeiture; descent of suicide's estate.

Section 16. Right of assembly; petition for redress of grievances.

Section 17. Standing army; necessity for legislative consent; subordination of military.

Section 18. Prohibition against quartering soldiers in homes.

Section 19. Hereditary distinctions; holding office during good behavior;
offices and titles from foreign states.

Section 20. Right to keep and bear arms.

ARTICLE II: LEGISLATURE – Page 32

Section 1. General Assembly to hold legislative power; composition.

Section 2. Composition of House and Senate; terms of office; districts; election.

Section 2A. Additional representative districts.

Section 2B. Delegates to Constitutional Convention.

Section 3. Qualifications of members.

Section 4. Time and frequency of sessions.

Section 5. Place of meeting.

Section 6. Vacancies; tenure of office of persons elected to fill.

Section 7. President pro tempore, Speaker and other officers; absence of presiding officers.

Section 8. Each House as judge of elections and qualifications of its members; quorum; adjournments; compelling attendance.

Section 9. Rules; punishment and expulsion of members; scope of powers.

Section 10. Journals; publication; entry of yeas and nays; passage of bills and resolutions.

Section 11. Accessibility to each House and Committees of the Whole.

Section 12. Consent of each House to adjournment.

Section 13. Immunity from arrest and questioning of speeches.

Section 14. Holding dual office or having interest in army or navy contract.

Section 15. Compensation, expenses and allowances of members.

Section 16. Restriction of bills and resolutions to one subject; expression in title; exception.

Section 17. Lotteries and other gambling.

Section 17A. Bingo games; organizations authorized to conduct; submission to referendum; districts; regulation; penalties.

Section 17B. Lotteries not under State control; organizations authorized to conduct; submission to referendum; districts; regulation; penalties.

Section 18. Divorce or alimony.

Section 19. Local or special laws relating to fences, livestock, ditches, school districts, and roads, highways, streets, etc.

Section 20. Disclosure of personal or private interest of legislator in any pending measure.

Section 21. Conviction of crime as ban to public office.

Section 22. Bribery of executive, judicial or legislative officers.

Section 23. Statutes as public laws unless otherwise declared.

Section 24. Settlement of accounts of State Treasurer; ineligibility for legislative office until settlement.

Section 25. Laws permitting zoning ordinances and use of land.

ARTICLE III: EXECUTIVE – Page 53

Section 1. Governor to be supreme executive.

Section 2. Election of Governor.

Section 3. Election returns, publications; election by General Assembly.

Section 4. Contested elections of Governor or Lieutenant-Governor.

Section 5. Term of office.

Section 6. Qualifications.

Section 7. Compensation.

Section 8. Governor as commander-in-chief of state armed forces.

Section 9. Appointing power; recess appointments; confirmation.

Section 10. Secretary of State; appointment, term, duties and compensation.

Section 11. County officers; qualifications; members of Congress, federal employees and other officers holding dual office.

Section 12. Commissions.

Section 13. Removal of officers by Governor; procedure.

Section 14. Reports from executive departments.

Section 15. Messages to General Assembly.

Section 16. Special sessions of General Assembly; adjournment; special session of Senate.

Section 17. Execution of laws.

Section 18. Approval or veto of bills, orders, resolutions or votes; repassage over veto.

Section 19. Lieutenant-Governor; election, term and qualifications; President of the Senate; compensation.

Section 20. Vacancy in offices of both Governor and Lieutenant-Governor; officers eligible to act; disability of Governor.

Section 21. Election and term of office for certain state officers.

Section 22. Election and term of office of certain county officers; commission.

Section 23. Place of office of certain county officers.

Section 24. Abolition of office of Clerk of Orphans' Court; transfer of functions.

ARTICLE IV: JUDICIARY – Page 63

Section 1. Creation of courts.

Section 2. Justices of Supreme Court and other State Judges; qualifications; residence; precedence.

Section 3. Appointment of judges; terms of office; vacancies; political representation; confirmation of appointment.

Section 4. Compensation of judges; method of payment; receipt of other fees or holding other office.

Section 5. Composition of Superior Court; presiding judge; quorum.

Section 6. Sessions of Superior Court.

Section 7. Jurisdiction of Superior Court.

Section 7A. Jurisdiction of Family Court.

Section 7B. Jurisdiction of Court of Common Pleas.

Section 8. Definitions of particular terms.

Section 9. Jurisdiction of Orphans' Court.

Section 10. Composition and jurisdiction of Court of Chancery; initiation and decisions in causes and proceedings.

Section 11. Jurisdiction of Supreme Court.

Section 12. Composition of Supreme Court; designation of temporary Justices; quorum; opening and adjourning court.

Section 13. Administrative head of courts; supervisory powers; designation of judges to sit in Court of Chancery, or the Superior Court.

Section 14. Power of law judges to grant restraining orders and preliminary injunctions.

Section 15. Judges ad litem; limitation and expiration of commission; compensation; persons not disqualified.

Section 16. Scope of jurisdiction and process; costs.

Section 17. Jurisdictional changes by General Assembly; appeals to Supreme Court.

Section 18. Powers of Chancellor, Vice-Chancellors and Judges.

Section 19. Instructions to jury.

Section 20. Trial by court of issues of fact in civil causes.

Section 21. Amendments in civil pleadings and proceedings by Superior Court; examination of witnesses and parties.

Section 22. Payment into court pending action for debt or damages; costs.

Section 23. Survival of action; executor or administrator as party; continuance.

Section 24. Security for stay of proceedings on appeal or writ of error.

Section 25. Chief Register in Chancery: appointment; powers and duties.

Section 26. Prothonotary as Clerk of Superior Court; powers and duties; entry of testatum fieri facias.

Section 27. Clerk of Supreme Court; term of office and compensation.

Section 28. Criminal jurisdiction of inferior courts and justices of the peace; regulation of jurisdiction; indictment; jury trial; appeals.

Section 29. Justices of the peace; term of office; powers of the Chief Magistrate and Justices of the Peace.

Section 30. Justices of the peace, Chief Magistrate, and judges of legislative courts; appointment by Governor; terms of office.

Section 31. Registers of Wills; depositions of witnesses; process; appeals to Court of Chancery; disqualification of Register for interest.

Section 32. Adjustment and settlement of executors' and administrators' accounts; notice; hearing of exceptions in Court of Chancery; transfer of jurisdiction; appeals.

Section 33. Style of process and public acts; prosecutions in name of State.

Section 34. Continuation in office and designation of certain judicial officers.

Section 34A. Continuation in office and designation of judicial officers of the Family Court and the Court of Common Pleas.

Section 35. Proceedings pending at time of 1951 amendment; books, records and papers; effect of amended article on Court of Chancery.

Section 36. Abolition of Orphans' Court; transfer of jurisdiction and powers.

Section 37. Court on the Judiciary.

Section 38. Retired Judges and Justices; temporary assignment.

Section 39. Senior judges.

ARTICLE V: ELECTIONS – Page 85

Section 1. Time and manner of holding general election.

Section 2. Qualifications for voting; members of the Armed Services of the United States stationed within State; persons disqualified; forfeiture of right.

Section 2A. Residence requirements in case of intrastate removal; election of President and Vice-President of United States; qualifications.

Section 2B. Residence requirements of persons from other states; election of President and Vice-President of United States; qualifications.

Section 3. Influencing voter; loss of vote; challenge; oath and affirmation; perjury.

Section 4. Registration of voters; days for registration; application to strike name from list; appeals; registration as prerequisite for voting.

Section 4A. General laws for absentee voting.

Section 4B. Uniform laws for absentee registration.

Section 5. Electors privileged from arrest; exceptions.

Section 6. Voting machine recording tapes, voting machine certificate, and absentee ballots; delivery to Prothonotary; duties and composition of court; quorum.

Section 7. Election offenses; penalties; self-incrimination.

Section 8. Prosecution for election offenses; procedure; appeal; bond.

Section 9. Enumeration of election offenses as limitation on power of General Assembly.

ARTICLE VI: IMPEACHMENT AND TREASON – Page 97

Section 1. Impeachment power of House; trial by Senate; oath of Senators; vote; presiding officers.

Section 2. Grounds for impeachment.

Section 3. Treason.

ARTICLE VII: PARDONS – Page 98

Section 1. Power of Governor; recommendation of Board of Pardons; entry in register and submission to General Assembly.

Section 2. Composition of Board of Pardons.

Section 3. Information from Attorney General on Board's duties.

ARTICLE VIII: REVENUE AND TAXATION - Page 99

Section 1. Uniformity of taxes; collection under general laws; exemption for public welfare purposes.

Section 2. Revenue bills to originate in House; amendments by Senate; restriction on definition; exclusion of unrelated matter.

Section 3. Borrowing money; specification of purpose; surplus borrowed money.

Section 4. Restrictions on loan of public money or bonds and credit of State.

Section 5. Capitation tax; uniformity; use.

Section 6. Procedure in withdrawal and payment of public moneys; annual publication of receipts and expenditures; limitation upon appropriations.

Section 7. Real estate assessments; inclusion of values.

Section 8. Lending credit, appropriating money to or becoming interested in any private corporation, person or company by county or municipality.

Section 9. Retroactive increase of taxation of personal income.

Section 10. Limitation on increase of rate of taxes and license fees; exception to meet obligation under faith and credit pledge; allocation of public moneys to meet such obligation if revenues are not sufficient to meet such pledge.

Section 11. Imposition or levy of new taxes or license fees.

Section 12. The Transportation Trust Fund; use and restrictions.

ARTICLE IX: CORPORATIONS – Page 107

Section 1. Creation, amendment, renewal or revival by general law; exceptions; revocation or forfeitures of charters; requisites for enactment of corporation laws.

Section 2. Acceptance of Constitution by existing corporations as prerequisite for amendment or renewal of charter.

Section 3. Issuance of stock.

Section 4. Rights, privileges, immunities and estates.

Section 5. Designation, by foreign corporation, of agent for service of process.

Section 6. Taxation of stock owned by persons or corporations without the State.

ARTICLE X: EDUCATION – Page 109

Section 1. Establishment and maintenance of free public schools; attendance.

Section 2. Annual appropriations; apportionment; use of funds; separation of schools; other expenses.

Section 3. Use of educational funds by religious schools; exemption of school property from taxation.

Section 4. Use of Public School Fund.

Section 5. Transportation of nonpublic school students.

Section 6. Property tax; use limitations.

ARTICLE XI: AGRICULTURE – Page 111

Section 1. State Board of Agriculture.

Section 2. Composition of Board; residence of Commissioners; quorum.

Section 3. Appointment of Commissioners by Governor; tenure; vacancies.

Section 4. Abatement and prevention of diseases of fruit trees, plants, vegetables, cereals and livestock.

Section 5. Plans for securing immigration of industrious and useful settlers.

Section 6. Compensation of Board members.

Section 7. Duration of Board.

18

ARTICLE XII: REPEALED – Page 113

Section 1. State Board of Health; local boards; powers / Repealed.

ARTICLE XIII: LOCAL OPTION – 114

Section 1. Submission of liquor question to district electors; election.

Section 2. Designation of districts for purposes of article.

Section 3. Laws for enforcement, manufacture and sale, and penalties.

ARTICLE XIV: OATH OF OFFICE - 115

Section 1. Form of oath for members of General Assembly and public officers.

ARTICLE XV: MISCELLANEOUS – Page 116

Section 1. Conservators of the peace.

Section 2. Receipt for fees.

Section 3. Costs on bill returned ignoramus or on acquittal.

Section 4. Extension of term of public officer; diminution of salary or emoluments.

Section 5. Officers to hold office until successors qualify.

Section 6. Behavior of officers; removal for misbehavior or infamous crime.

Section 7. Offenses excepted from prohibition against prosecuting by information and jury trial.

Section 8. Interest of member or officer of department in contracts for supplies or services of department prohibited.

Section 9. Prefixing Constitution to codification of laws.

Section 10. Disqualification to hold office by reason of sex.

ARTICLE XVI: AMENDMENTS AND CONVENTIONS – Page 118

Section 1. Proposal of Constitutional amendments in General Assembly; procedure.

Section 2. Constitutional Conventions; procedure; compensation of delegates; quorum; powers and duties; vacancies.

Section 3. Receiving, tallying and counting votes for or against Convention; return of vote; enabling legislation.

Section 4. Approval of bills or resolutions under this article; exemption from

Section 5. Separate ballots on question of Convention.

ARTICLE XVII: CONTINUITY OF GOVERNMENTAL OPERATIONS - 120

Section 1. Continuity of state and local governmental operations in periods of emergency resulting from disasters caused by enemy attack.

SCHEDULE – Page 121

Section 1. Delivery, filing and publication of enrolled copy of amended Constitution and Schedule.

Section 2. Effective date of amended Constitution.

Section 3. Effect on offices of Senators and Representatives; election.

Section 4. Commencement of terms of members of General Assembly.

Section 5. Date of first general election.

Section 6. Effect on Governor's term.

Section 7. Continuation of elective and appointive offices; election of successors; renewal of official obligations.

Section 8. Date of commencement of terms of elective officers.

Section 9. Date of abolition of courts and judicial offices; transfer of pending proceedings and books, records and papers.

Section 10. Registers' Court and jurisdiction of justice of the peace unaffected.

Section 11. Payments to certain incumbent judges not reappointed.

Section 12. First biennial session of General Assembly under Constitution.

Section 13. Exceptions to limitations on amount of compensation payable to members of General Assembly and presiding officers.

Section 14. Renewal of existing corporations until enactment of general incorporation law.

Section 15. Guardians' accounts.

Section 16. Terms of office of persons holding office on effective date of Constitution.

Section 17. Vacancies in Board of Pardons.

Section 18. Laws consistent with Constitution not affected.

Section 19. Enabling legislation.

PREAMBLE

Through Divine goodness, all people have by nature the rights of worshiping and serving their Creator according to the dictates of their consciences, of enjoying and defending life and liberty, of acquiring and protecting reputation and property, and in general of obtaining objects suitable to their condition, without injury by one to another; and as these rights are essential to their welfare, for due exercise thereof, power is inherent in them; and therefore all just authority in the institutions of political society is derived from the people, and established with their consent, to advance their happiness; and they may for this end, as circumstances require, from time to time, alter their Constitution of government.

ARTICLE I: BILL OF RIGHTS

Section 1. Freedom of religion.
Although it is the duty of all persons frequently to assemble together for the public worship of Almighty God; and piety and morality, on which the prosperity of communities depends, are hereby promoted; yet no person shall or ought to be compelled to attend any religious worship, to contribute to the erection or support of any place of worship, or to the maintenance of any ministry, against his or her own free will and consent; and no power shall or ought to be vested in or assumed by any magistrate that shall in any case interfere with, or in any manner control the rights of conscience, in the free exercise of religious worship, nor a preference given by law to any religious societies, denominations, or modes of worship.

Section 2. Religious test for office not required.
No religious test shall be required as a qualification to any office, or public trust, under this State.

Section 3. Free and equal elections.
All elections shall be free and equal.

Section 4. Trial by jury.
Trial by jury shall be as heretofore.

Section 5. Freedom of press and speech; evidence in libel prosecutions; jury questions.
The free communication of thoughts and opinions is one of the invaluable rights of man. The press shall be free to every citizen who undertakes to examine the official conduct of persons acting in a public capacity; and any citizen may freely speak, write and print on any subject, being responsible for the abuse of that liberty. In prosecutions for publications, investigating the proceedings of officers, or where the matter published is proper for public information, the truth thereof may be given in evidence; and in all indictments for libels the jury may determine the facts and the law, as in other cases.

Section 6. Searches and seizures.
The people shall be secure in their persons, houses, papers and possessions, from unreasonable searches and seizures; and no warrant to search any place, or to seize any person or thing, shall issue without describing them as particularly as may be; nor then, unless there be probable cause supported by oath or affirmation.

Section 7. Procedural rights in criminal prosecutions; jury trial; self-incrimination; deprivation of life, liberty or property.
In all criminal prosecutions, the accused hath a right to be heard by himself or herself and his or her counsel, to be plainly and fully informed of the nature and cause of the accusation against him or her, to meet the witnesses in their examination face to face, to have compulsory process in due time, on application by himself or herself, his or her friends or counsel, for obtaining witnesses in his or her favor, and a speedy and public trial by an impartial jury; he or she shall not be compelled to give evidence against himself or herself, nor shall he or she be deprived of life, liberty or property, unless by the judgment of his or her peers or by the law of the land.

Section 8. Prosecution by indictment or information; double jeopardy; just compensation for property.
No person shall for any indictable offense be proceeded against criminally by information, except in cases arising in the land or naval forces, or in the militia when in actual service in time of war or public danger; and no person shall be for the same offense twice put in jeopardy of life or limb; nor shall any person's property be taken or applied to public use without the consent of his or her representatives, and without compensation being made.

Section 9. Courts shall be open; remedy for injury; suits against State.

All courts shall be open; and every person for an injury done him or her in his or her reputation, person, movable or immovable possessions, shall have remedy by the due course of law, and justice administered according to the very right of the cause and the law of the land, without sale, denial, or unreasonable delay or expense. Suits may be brought against the State, according to such regulations as shall be made by law.

Section 10. Suspension of laws by General Assembly.

No power of suspending laws shall be exercised but by authority of the General Assembly.

Section 11. Excessive bail or fines; cruel punishments; health of prisoners.

Excessive bail shall not be required, nor excessive fines imposed, nor cruel punishments inflicted; and in the construction of jails a proper regard shall be had to the health of prisoners.

Section 12. Right to bail; access to accused.

All prisoners shall be bailable by sufficient sureties, unless for capital offenses when the proof is positive or the presumption great; and when persons are confined on accusation for such offenses their friends and counsel may at proper seasons have access to them.

Section 13. Suspension of habeas corpus.

The privilege of the writ of habeas corpus shall not be suspended, unless when in cases of rebellion or invasion the public safety may require it.

Section 14. Commission of oyer and terminer, or jail delivery.

No commission of oyer and terminer, or jail delivery, shall be issued.

Section 15. Corruption of blood; forfeiture; descent of suicide's estate.
No attainder shall work corruption of blood, nor except during the life of the offender forfeiture of estate. The estates of those who destroy their own lives shall descend or vest as in case of natural death, and if any person be killed by accident no forfeiture shall thereby be incurred.

Section 16. Right of assembly; petition for redress of grievances.
Although disobedience to laws by a part of the people, upon suggestions of impolicy or injustice in them, tends by immediate effect and the influence of example not only to endanger the public welfare and safety, but also in governments of a republican form contravenes the social principles of such governments, founded on common consent for common good; yet the citizens have a right in an orderly manner to meet together, and to apply to persons intrusted with the powers of government, for redress of grievances or other proper purposes, by petition, remonstrance or address.

Section 17. Standing army; necessity for legislative consent; subordination of military.
No standing army shall be kept without the consent of the General Assembly, and the military shall in all cases and at all times be in strict subordination to the civil power.

Section 18. Prohibition against quartering soldiers in homes.
No soldier shall in time of peace be quartered in any house without the consent of the owner; not in time of war but by a civil magistrate, in manner to be prescribed by law.

Section 19. Hereditary distinctions; holding office during good behavior; offices and titles from foreign states.
No hereditary distinction shall be granted, nor any office created or exercised, the appointment to which shall be for a longer term than during good behaviour; and no person holding any office

under this State shall accept of any office or title of any kind whatever from any king, prince, or foreign State.

Section 20. Right to keep and bear arms.
A person has the right to keep and bear arms for the defense of self, family, home and State, and for hunting and recreational use.

WE DECLARE THAT EVERYTHING IN THIS ARTICLE IS RESERVED OUT OF THE GENERAL POWERS OF GOVERNMENT HEREINAFTER MENTIONED.

ARTICLE II: LEGISLATURE

Section 1. General Assembly to hold legislative power; composition.

Section 1. The legislative power of this State shall be vested in a General Assembly, which shall consist of a Senate and House of Representatives.

Section 2. Composition of House and Senate; terms of office; districts; election.

The House of Representatives shall be composed of thirty-five members, plus such additional members as shall be provided pursuant to Section 2A of this Article, who shall be chosen for two years. The Senate shall be composed of twenty-one members, who shall be chosen for four years.

The State is hereby divided into thirty-five Representative Districts. There shall be such additional Representative Districts as shall be provided pursuant to Section 2A of this Article. From each Representative District there shall be chosen, by the qualified electors thereof, one Representative. The State is also hereby divided into twenty-one Senatorial Districts, from each of which shall be chosen, by the qualified electors thereof, one Senator. In New Castle County there shall be seven Senatorial Districts, numbered from one to seven inclusive; in Kent County, seven Senatorial Districts, numbered from one to seven inclusive; and in Sussex County, seven Senatorial Districts from one to seven inclusive.

The Representative Districts in New Castle County are and shall be as follows:

Number One. All that portion of the City of Wilmington included within the Second and Fourth Wards, and those parts of the Sixth and Eighth Wards, respectively, lying south of and bounded by the central line of Eighth street.

Number Two. All that portion of the said city included within the Ninth Ward, and those parts of the Sixth and Eighth Wards, respectively, lying north of and bounded by the central line of Eighth street.

Number Three. All that portion of the said city included within the Seventh Ward, and that part of the Fifth Ward lying north of and bounded by a straight line including the central line of Eighth street.

Number Four. All that portion of the said city included within the First and Third Wards, and that part of the Fifth Ward lying south of and bounded by the central line of Eighth street, east of and bounded by the central line of Adams street, and west of and bounded by the central line of Market street.

Number Five. All that portion of the said city included within the Tenth, Eleventh and Twelfth Wards, and that part of the Fifth Ward lying south of and bounded by a straight line including the central line of Eighth street, west of and bounded by the central line of Adams street, and bounded on the west by the westerly boundary line of the said city.

Number Six. Brandywine Hundred.

Number Seven. Christiana Hundred.

Number Eight. Mill Creek Hundred.

Number Nine. White Clay Creek Hundred.

Number Ten. New Castle Hundred.

Number Eleven. Pencader Hundred.

Number Twelve. Red Lion Hundred.

Number Thirteen. St. Georges Hundred.

Number Fourteen. Appoquinimink Hundred.

Number Fifteen. Blackbird Hundred.
The Representative Districts in Kent County are and shall be as follows:

Number One. Duck Creek Hundred.

Number Two. Little Creek Hundred and the first Election District of East Dover Hundred.

Number Three. Kenton Hundred.

Number Four. West Dover Hundred and all that portion of East Dover Hundred lying next to West Dover Hundred and separate from the rest of East Dover Hundred by the following boundary lines: beginning at the middle of the public road leading from the Horsehead road to Kenton at the point of intersection of Kenton Hundred and East Dover Hundred, thence running along the middle of the said road to the Horsehead road, thence running in a westerly direction along the middle of the said Horsehead road a short distance to a short road leading from the said Horsehead road to the road from Dover to Hazlettville, known as the Hazlettville road, thence running along the middle of the said short road from the Horsehead road to the said Hazlettville road, thence running in a westerly direction along the middle of the said Hazlettville road a short distance to the road leading therefrom to Wyoming, thence running along the middle of the said road leading from the said Hazlettville road to Wyoming to the point of intersection of East Dover Hundred and North Murderkill Hundred.

Number Five. All that portion of East Dover Hundred not included in Districts numbers two and four.

Number Six. Parts of North Murderkill, South Murderkill and Mispillion Hundreds included within the following boundary lines: beginning at the intersection of the southern line of South Murderkill Hundred with the State of Maryland, thence running along the division line between Mispillion Hundred and South Murderkill Hundred to the public road leading from Whiteleysburg to Harrington, thence running in a southeasterly and easterly direction along the middle of said public road to the public road leading from Masten's Corner to Vernon, at or near White's Church, thence running in a northeasterly direction along the middle of said public road leading from Masten's Corner to Vernon, a short distance to the public road leading therefrom to the town of Harrington, being a continuation of the road leading from Whiteleysburg to Harrington, thence running in a southeasterly direction to the intersection of West street in the town of Harrington, thence running in a northerly direction along the middle of said West street to the middle of Wolcott street in said town of Harrington, thence running in an easterly direction along the middle of said Wolcott street to the middle of Dorman street in said town of Harrington, thence running in a northerly direction along the middle of said Dorman street to Brown's Branch, thence running in an easterly direction with the course of said Branch to the Delaware Railroad, thence running in a northerly direction along said Delaware Railroad to Beaver Dam Branch in South Murderkill Hundred, thence following the course of said Beaver Dam Branch in a northwesterly direction to the public road leading from Felton to Whiteleysburg, thence running in a northeasterly direction along the middle of the said public road from Felton to Whiteleysburg to the Owl's Nest road, thence running in a northerly direction along the middle of the said Owl's Nest road to the intersection of the Cowgill road from Woodside to Petersburg, thence running in a northerly direction along the middle of the said Cowgill road to the Reed road running from Woodside to DuPont's school house, thence running in a northwesterly direction along the middle of the said Reed road to DuPont's school house, thence running in a northerly direction along the middle of the public road leading from Willow Grove to Camden, a short distance to Stubb's

Corner, thence running in a westerly and northwesterly and westerly direction along the middle of the public road leading from DuPont's school house to the Almshouse to Gray's Corner, thence continuing in a direct westerly line to the southern boundary line of West Dover Hundred, thence following the southern boundary line of West Dover Hundred in a westerly direction to the State of Maryland, thence running in a southerly direction along the eastern boundary line to the State of Maryland to the place of beginning.

Number Seven. All that portion of North Murderkill Hundred not included in District number six.

Number Eight. All that portion of South Murderkill Hundred not included in District number six.

Number Nine. All that portion of Mispillion Hundred not included in District number six.

Number Ten. Milford Hundred.

The Representative Districts in Sussex County are and shall be as follows:

Number One. Cedar Creek Hundred.

Number Two. All that portion of Nanticoke Hundred which lies north and west of Gravelly Branch, beginning at a point where the said Gravelly Branch intersects the dividing line between Georgetown and Nanticoke Hundreds and running in a southwesterly course to what was formerly known as Rest's Old Mill, thence along said branch to what was formerly known as Collins' Mills, to its mouth being at the head of Middleford Mill Pond; together with North West Fork Hundred.

Number Three. All that portion of Nanticoke Hundred which lies south and east of said Gravelly Branch, beginning at a point where the said Gravelly Branch intersects the dividing line between Nanticoke and Georgetown Hundreds, running in a southwesterly course to what was formerly known as Rest's Old Mill, thence along said branch to what was formerly known as Collins' Mills, to its mouth at the head of Middleford Mill Pond; together with Seaford Hundred.

Number Four. Broad Creek Hundred.

Number Five. Little Creek Hundred.

Number Six. Dagsboro and Gumboro Hundreds.

Number Seven. Baltimore Hundred.

Number Eight. Indian River Hundred.

Number Nine. Georgetown Hundred.

Number Ten. Broadkiln and Lewes and Rehoboth Hundreds.

The Senatorial Districts in New Castle County are and shall be as follows:

Number One. All that portion of the City of Wilmington lying north of and bounded by a straight line including the central line of Eighth street extending from the Delaware River to the westerly boundary of said city.

Number Two. All that portion of the said City lying south of and bounded by the straight line aforesaid including the central line of Eighth street.

Number Three. Brandywine Hundred, together with all that portion of Christiana Hundred lying north of and bounded by the central line of Lancaster Turnpike.

Number Four. Milk Creek Hundred, together with all that portion of Christiana Hundred lying south of and bounded by the central line of the Lancaster Turnpike.

Number Five. White Clay Creek Hundred, Red Lion Hundred and New Castle Hundred.

Number Six. Pencader Hundred and St. Georges Hundred.

Number Seven. Appoquinimink Hundred and Blackbird Hundred.

The Senatorial Districts in Kent County are and shall be as follows:

Number One. The first and second Representative Districts.

Number Two. The third and fourth Representative Districts.

Number Three. The fifth and seventh Representative Districts.

Number Four. The sixth and ninth Representative Districts.

Number Five. The eighth and tenth Representative Districts.

Number Six, at Large. The first, second, fifth, seventh and eighth Representative Districts.

Number Seven, at Large. The third, fourth, sixth, ninth and tenth Representative Districts.

The Senatorial Districts in Sussex County are and shall be as follows:

Number One. The first and second Representative Districts.

Number Two. The third and fourth Representative Districts.

Number Three. The fifth and sixth Representative Districts.

Number Four. The seventh and eighth Representative Districts.

Number Five. The ninth and tenth Representative Districts.

Number Six, at Large. The first, second, third, fourth and fifth Representative Districts.

Number Seven, at Large. The sixth, seventh, eighth, ninth and tenth Representative Districts.

The first Senators elected from the Sixth Senatorial Districts of Kent and Sussex Counties shall serve for a two year term only, thereafter their successors shall serve for a full four year term.

All territory which shall hereafter be added to and included within the City of Wilmington shall become part of the Representative Districts in New Castle County, as follows:

All lying east of a straight line including the central line of Market street, below Eighth street, as the said two streets now exist, and south of a straight line including the central line of Eighth street, as the same now exists, shall become part of Representative District number one.

All lying north of a straight line including the central line of Eighth street, as the same now exists, extending from the northeasterly side of Brandywine Creek to the Delaware River, or north of the Brandywine Creek, westerly from the point of intersection of the said straight line with the northeasterly side of the said Creek, shall become part of Representative District number two.

All lying north of a straight line including the central line of Eighth street, as the same now exists, south of the Brandywine Creek, and west of the central line of Market street, as the same now exists, shall become part of Representative District number three.

All lying between a straight line including the central line of Market street extended southerly and a straight line including the central line of Washington street extended southerly shall become part of Representative District number four.

All lying south of a straight line including the central line of

Eighth street, as the same now exists, and west of a straight line including the central line of Washington street, as the same now exists, shall become part of Representative District number five.

In case of any change in the boundary line between this State and the State of Pennsylvania any of the said Senatorial and Representative Districts in New Castle County affected thereby shall conform to any new boundary line between the said States.

All territory which shall hereafter be added to and included within the City of Wilmington shall become part of the Senatorial Districts in New Castle County as follows:

All lying north of a straight line including the central line of Eighth street, extended from the Delaware River westwardly, shall become part of Senatorial District number one.

All lying south of a straight line including the central line of Eighth street, extended from the Delaware River westwardly shall become part of Senatorial District number two.

Whenever by the extension of the limits of the City of Wilmington territory forming part of any Representative or Senatorial District, as hereby established, shall be included within the limits of the said city, such Representative or Senatorial District shall thereafter consist of the residue thereof, not so included within said limits.

The several Representative and Senatorial Districts in the State shall, except as herein otherwise provided, continue to be bounded, described and defined by the lines of the hundreds, wards, election districts, public roads, railroad and other boundaries herein mentioned, as the same are now established and located.

Section 2A. Additional representative districts.
In addition to the existing 35 Representative Districts as set forth in Section 2 of this Article, there shall be additional Representative Districts as hereafter provided.
Each existing Representative District as set forth in Section 2 of this Article, with a population residing therein in excess of 15,000, as shown by the last official federal decennial census shall be entitled to one additional Representative for each additional 15,000 population or major fraction thereof residing within the District.

Upon any Representative District, as set forth in Section 2 of this Article, being entitled to more than one Representative, it shall be subdivided into new Representative Districts for each additional Representative to which it is entitled, from which shall be chosen by the qualified electors thereof, a Representative. After each official federal decennial census the new Representative Districts created pursuant to this Section shall be abolished and the Representative Districts set forth in Section 2 of this Article shall again be re-divided as set forth herein.
The sub-dividing of the Representative Districts as set forth herein shall be done by a Redistricting Commission, consisting of the Governor, as Chairman, and the State Chairman of the two political parties receiving the largest vote for Governor at the

preceding election for Governor as advisors to the Governor. Redistricting and reapportioning by the Commission as set forth herein shall be accomplished in accordance with the following criteria: Each new Representative District shall, insofar as is possible, be formed of contiguous territory; shall be as nearly equal in population as possible to the other new districts being created within the existing Representative District; shall be bounded by ancient boundaries, major roads, streams, or other natural boundaries; and not be so created as to unduly favor any person or political party.

Within 120 calendar days following the official reporting to the President of the United States of each decennial census, (or within 120 calendar days after this amendment takes effect) the Governor, on behalf of the Commission, shall file with the Secretary of State the plan for redistricting and reapportioning as provided for herein. Forthwith, after the filing, the Governor shall issue a proclamation of redistricting and reapportioning. The Secretary of State shall cause such proclamation to be published in two newspapers of general circulation within the State for two consecutive weeks, within 20 days after the issuance of the proclamation. The proclamation shall become effective within 30 days of its issuance.

Any qualified voter may apply to the Superior Court to compel the Governor, by mandamus or otherwise, to perform the redistricting and reapportioning duties or to correct any error in redistricting and reapportioning. Application to compel the Governor to perform the redistricting and reapportioning duties must be filed within thirty days of the expiration of the 120 days allotted to the Commission to file its plan, if such plan is not timely filed. Application to compel correction of any error in redistricting and reapportioning must be filed within thirty days following the proclamation. Original jurisdiction in these matters is hereby vested in the Superior Court. On appeal, the cause shall be reviewed by the Supreme Court upon the law and the facts.

Section 2B. Delegates to Constitutional Convention.
The number of delegates and the method of electing delegates to the Constitutional Convention as provided in Section 2, Article 16, shall not be effected by the addition of Representatives or Representative Districts, pursuant to Section 2A of this Article. The Representative Districts which shall elect delegates to the Constitutional Convention are as set forth in Section 2 of this Article.

Section 3. Qualifications of members.
No person shall be a Senator who shall not have attained the age of twenty-seven years and have been a citizen and inhabitant of the State three years next preceding the day of his or her election and the last year of that term an inhabitant of the Senatorial District in which he or she shall be chosen, unless he or she shall have been absent on the public business of the United States or of this State. No person shall be a Representative who shall not have attained the age of twenty-four years, and have been a citizen and inhabitant of the State three years next preceding the day of his or her election, and the last year of that term an inhabitant of the Representative District in which he or she shall be chosen, unless he or she shall have been absent on the public business of the United States or of this State.

Section 4. Time and frequency of sessions.
The General Assembly shall convene on the second Tuesday of January of each calendar year unless otherwise convened by the Governor, or by mutual call of the presiding officers of both Houses.

The General Assembly may continue in session each calendar year so long as, in its judgment, the public interest may require; however, each session shall not extend beyond the last day of June unless the session is recalled by the Governor or the mutual call of the presiding officers of both Houses.

Section 5. Place of meeting.

The General Assembly shall meet and sit in Dover, the capital of the State; provided, however, that in case of insurrection, conflagration or epidemic disease the General Assembly may temporarily meet and sit elsewhere.

Section 6. Vacancies; tenure of office of persons elected to fill.

Whenever there shall be a vacancy in either House of the General Assembly, by reason of failure to elect, ineligibility, death, resignation or otherwise, a writ of election shall be issued by the presiding officer of the House in which the vacancy exists, or in case of necessity in such other manner as shall be provided by law; and the person thereupon chosen to fill such vacancy shall hold office for the residue of the term. And whenever there shall be such vacancy in either House, and the General Assembly is not in session, the Governor shall have power to issue a writ of election to fill such vacancy, which writ shall be executed as a writ issued by the presiding officer of either House in case of vacancy, and the person thereupon chosen to fill such vacancy shall hold office for the residue of the term.

Section 7. President pro tempore, Speaker and other officers; absence of presiding officers.

The Senate at the first annual session of every new General Assembly shall choose one of its members president pro tempore, who shall preside in the absence of the Lieutenant-Governor, or in case the latter shall become Governor or while he or she continues in the exercise of the office of Governor by reason of disability of the Governor. The Senate shall also choose its other officers and in the absence of the Lieutenant-Governor and its president pro tempore may, from time to time, as occasion may require, appoint one of its members to preside. The House of Representatives at such first annual session shall choose one of its members speaker and also choose its other officers, and in the absence of the speaker may from time to time, as occasion may require, appoint one of its members to preside.

Section 8 Each House as judge of elections and qualifications of its members; quorum; adjournments; compelling attendance.

Each House shall be the judge of the elections, returns and qualifications of its own members; and a majority of all the members elected to each House shall constitute a quorum to do business; but a smaller number may adjourn from day to day, and shall have power to compel the attendance of absent members, in such manner and under such penalties, as shall be deemed expedient.

Section 9. Rules; punishment and expulsion of members; scope of powers.

Each House may determine the rules of its proceedings, punish any of its members for disorderly behavior, and with the concurrence of two-thirds of all the members elected thereto expel a member, and shall have all other powers necessary for a branch of the Legislature of a free and independent State.

Section 10. Journals; publication; entry of yeas and nays; passage of bills and resolutions.

Each House shall keep a journal of its proceedings, and publish the same immediately after every session, except such parts as may require secrecy. The names of the members voting for and against any bill or joint resolution, except in relation to adjournment, shall on the final vote be entered on the journal; and the yeas and nays of the members on any question shall, at the desire of any member, be entered on the journal. No bill or joint resolution, except in relation to adjournment, shall pass either House unless the final vote shall have been taken by yeas and nays, nor without the concurrence of a majority of all the members elected to each House.

Section 11. Accessibility to each House and Committees of the Whole.
The doors of each House, and of Committees of the Whole, shall be open unless when the business is such as ought to be kept secret.

Section 12. Consent of each House to adjournment.
Neither House shall, without the consent of the other, adjourn for more than three days, nor to any other place than that in which the two Houses shall be sitting.

Section 13. Immunity from arrest and questioning of speeches.
The Senators and Representatives shall, in all cases, except treason, felony or breach of the peace, be privileged from arrest during their attendance at the session of their respective Houses, and in going to and returning from the same; and for any speech or debate in either House they shall not be questioned in any other place.

Section 14. Holding dual office or having interest in army or navy contract.
No Senator or Representative shall, during the time for which he or she shall have been elected, be appointed to any civil office under this State which shall have been created, or the emoluments of which shall have been increased during such time. No member of Congress, nor any person holding any office under this State, or the United States, except officers usually appointed by the courts of justice respectively, attorneys-at-law and officers of the militia, holding no disqualifying office, shall during his or her continuance in Congress or in office be a Senator or Representative; nor shall any person while concerned in any army or navy contract be a Senator or Representative.

Section 15. Compensation, expenses and allowances of members.
The President of the Senate and members of the General Assembly shall receive an annual salary and an annual expense allowance for transportation and such other necessary and proper purposes as the General Assembly shall by law provide. Funds appropriated hereunder shall be paid out of the Treasury of the State.

Section 16. Restriction of bills and resolutions to one subject; expression in title; exception.
No bill or joint resolution, except bills appropriating money for public purposes, shall embrace more than one subject, which shall be expressed in its title.

Section 17. Lotteries and other gambling.
All forms of gambling are prohibited in this State except the following:

(a) Lotteries under State control for the purpose of raising funds,
(b) Lotteries (other than slot machines, roulette, craps and baccarat games) provided that each is sponsored and conducted under the limitations of Section 17B by companies, organizations or societies which have been in existence for at least 2 years; provided, however, that no person who shall not have attained the age of 18 years shall participate in any lottery (where money is the prize) otherwise authorized by the article,
(c) Wagering or betting by the use of pari-mutuel machines or totalizators on horse races conducted at racetracks within or without the State, provided that such wagering or betting may be conducted only either:

(1) within the enclosure of any racetrack licensed under the laws of the State to conduct a race meeting, or
(2) within the enclosure of any racetrack licensed under the laws of the State to receive and accept wagers or bets on electronically televised simulcasts of horse races.

(d) Bingo games as conducted under the limitations of Section 17A.

The General Assembly shall enforce this Section by appropriate legislation.

Section 17A. Bingo games; organizations authorized to conduct;
submission to referendum; districts; regulation; penalties.

The game of Bingo shall be lawful when sponsored and conducted by Volunteer Fire Companies, Veterans' Organizations, Religious or Charitable Organizations, or by Fraternal Societies provided the net receipts or profits arising from the conducting or operating of such Bingo games by the aforementioned Companies, Organizations, or Societies are used solely for the promotion or achievement of the purposes of such Companies, Organizations, or Societies, and provided further that the aforementioned Companies, Organizations or Societies are operated in a manner so as to come within the provisions of Section 170 of the U. S. Revenue Code and Regulations promulgated thereunder by the U. S. Secretary of the Treasury.

1. The General Assembly shall provide by law for the submission to the vote of the qualified electors of the several districts of the State, or any of them, mentioned in subparagraph 2 of Section 17A of this article at the General Election held in 1958, the question whether the playing of the game of "Bingo" shall be licensed or prohibited within the limits thereof; and in every district in which there is a majority against license, no organization, mentioned in Section 17A, shall thereafter sponsor or permit the playing of "Bingo", within said district, until at a subsequent submission of such question a majority of votes shall be cast in said district for license. Whenever a majority of all the members elected to each House of the General Assembly by the qualified electors in any district named in subparagraph 2 of Section 17A of this Article shall request the submission of the question of license or no license to a vote of the qualified electors in said district, the General Assembly shall provide for the submission of such question to the qualified electors in such district at the next general election thereafter.

2. Under the provisions of this Article, Sussex County shall comprise one district, Kent County shall comprise one district, the City of Wilmington, as its corporate limits now are or may hereafter be extended, one district, and the remaining part of New Castle County, one district.

3. The General Assembly shall provide necessary laws to carry out and enforce the provisions of this Article, enact laws governing the game of "Bingo" under the limitations of this Article, and may provide such penalties as may be necessary to enforce same.

Section 17B. Lotteries not under State control; organizations authorized to conduct; submission to referendum; districts; regulation; penalties.

Lotteries not under State control shall be lawful when sponsored and conducted by volunteer fire companies, veterans organizations, religious or charitable organizations, or by fraternal societies provided that said company, organization or society has been in existence a minimum of 2 years and provided the net receipts or profits arising from the conducting or operating of such lotteries by the aforementioned companies, organizations or societies are used solely for the promotion or achievement of the purposes of such companies, organizations or societies, and provided further that the aforementioned companies, organizations or societies are operated in a manner so as to come within Section 170 of the United States Revenue Code and regulations promulgated thereunder by the United States Secretary of the Treasury.

1. The General Assembly shall provide by law for the submission to the vote of the qualified electors of the several districts of the State, or any of them, mentioned in paragraph 2 of this section at the general election held in 1984, the question whether the playing of lotteries not under State control shall be licensed or prohibited within the limits thereof; and in every district in which there is a majority against license, no organization, mentioned in this section, shall thereafter sponsor or permit lotteries not under State control, within said district, until at a subsequent submission of such question a majority of votes shall be cast in said district for license. Whenever a majority of all the members elected to each House of the General Assembly by the qualified electors in any district named in paragraph 2 of this section shall request the submission of the question of license or no license to a vote of the qualified electors in said district, the General Assembly shall provide for the submission of such question to the qualified electors in such district at the next general election thereafter.

2. Under this article, Sussex County shall comprise 1 district, Kent County shall comprise 1 district, the City of Wilmington, as its corporate limits now are or may hereafter be extended, 1 district, and the remaining part of New Castle County, 1 district.

3. The General Assembly shall enact comprehensive legislation providing for licensing for all organizations conducting and regulating the conduct of lotteries under this section and may provide such penalties as may be necessary to enforce such legislation.

Section 18. Divorce or alimony.

No divorce shall be granted, nor alimony allowed, except by the judgment of a court, as shall be prescribed by general and uniform law.

Section 19. Local or special laws relating to fences, livestock, ditches, school districts, and roads, highways, streets, etc.

The General Assembly shall not pass any local or special law relating to fences; the straying of livestock; ditches; the creation or changing the boundaries of school districts; or the laying out, opening, alteration, maintenance or vacation, in whole or in part of any road, highway, street, lane or alley; provided, however, that the General Assembly may by a vote of two-thirds of all the members elected to each House pass laws relating to the laying out, opening, alteration or maintenance of any road or highway which forms a continuous road or highway extending through at least a portion of the three counties of the State.

No road, highway or street, intended to be dedicated to public use and maintained at public expense, shall be constructed except in conformance with standards adopted by the agency charged with construction, reconstruction or maintenance of such road, highway or street. Any road or street constructed solely for private use shall only be maintained at State expense after it has been constructed or reconstructed according to the standards established by the agency charged with the duty of maintaining such roads or streets.

Section 20. Disclosure of personal or private interest of legislator in any pending measure.
Any member of the General Assembly who has a personal or private interest in any measure or bill pending in the General Assembly shall disclose the fact to the House of which he or she is a member and shall not vote thereon.

Section 21. Conviction of crime as ban to public office.
No person who shall be convicted of embezzlement of the public money, bribery, perjury or other infamous crime, shall be eligible to a seat in either House of the General Assembly, or capable of holding any office of trust, honor or profit under this State.

Section 22. Bribery of executive, judicial or legislative officers.
Every person who shall give, offer or promise, directly or indirectly, any money, testimonial, privilege, personal advantage or thing of value to any executive or judicial officer of this State or to any member of either House of the General Assembly for the purpose of influencing him or her in the performance of any of his or her official or public duties shall be deemed guilty of bribery, and shall be punished in such manner as shall be provided by law.

Section 23. Statutes as public laws unless otherwise declared.

Every statute shall be a public law unless otherwise declared in the statute itself.

Section 24. Settlement of accounts of State Treasurer; ineligibility for legislative office until settlement.

The State Treasurer shall settle his or her accounts annually with the General Assembly or a joint committee thereof, which shall be appointed at every ninety legislative day session. No person who has served in the office of State Treasurer shall be eligible to a seat in either House of the General Assembly until he or she shall have made a final settlement of his or her accounts as treasurer and discharged the balance, if any, due thereon.

Section 25. Laws permitting zoning ordinances and use of land.

The General Assembly may enact laws under which municipalities and the County of Sussex and the County of Kent and the County of New Castle may adopt zoning ordinances, laws or rules limiting and restricting to specified districts and regulating therein buildings and structures according to their construction and the nature and extent of their use, as well as the use to be made of land in such districts for other than agricultural purposes; and the exercise of such authority shall be deemed to be within the police power of the State.

ARTICLE III: EXECUTIVE

Section 1. Governor to be supreme executive.
The supreme executive powers of the State shall be vested in a Governor.

Section 2. Election of Governor.
The Governor shall be chosen by the qualified electors of the State, once in every four years, at the general election.

Section 3. Election returns, publications; election by General Assembly.
The returns of every election for Governor shall be sealed up and immediately transmitted to the President of the Senate, or in case of a vacancy in the office of President of the Senate, or his or her absence from the State to the Secretary of State, who shall keep the same until a President of the Senate shall be chosen, to whom they shall be immediately transmitted after his or her election, who shall open and publish the same in the presence of the members of both Houses of the General Assembly. Duplicates of the said returns shall also be immediately lodged with the Prothonotary of each county. The person having the highest number of votes shall be Governor; but if two or more shall be equal in the highest number of votes, the members of the two Houses shall, by joint ballot, choose one of them to be Governor; and if, upon such ballot, two or more of them shall still be equal and highest in votes, the President of the Senate shall have the casting vote.

Section 4. Contested elections of Governor or Lieutenant-Governor.
Contested elections of the Governor or Lieutenant-Governor shall be determined by a joint committee, consisting of one-third of all the members elected to each House of the General Assembly, to be selected by ballot of the Houses respectively. Every member of the committee shall take an oath or affirmation that in determining the said election he or she will faithfully discharge the trust reposed in him or her; and the committee shall always

sit with open doors.

The Chief Justice, or, in case of his or her absence or disability, the Chancellor shall preside at the trial of any contested election of Governor or Lieutenant-Governor, and shall decide questions regarding the admissibility of evidence, and shall, upon request of the committee, pronounce his or her opinion upon other questions of law involved in the trial.

Section 5. Term of office.
The Governor shall hold his or her office during four years from the third Tuesday in January next ensuing his or her election; and shall not be elected a third time to said office.

Section 6. Qualifications.
The Governor shall be at least thirty years of age, and have been a citizen and inhabitant of the United States twelve years next before the day of his or her election, and the last six years of that term an inhabitant of this State, unless he or she shall have been absent on public business of the United States or of this State.

Section 7. Compensation.
The Governor shall, at stated times, receive for his or her services an adequate salary to be fixed by law, which shall be neither increased nor diminished during the period for which he or she shall have been elected.

Section 8. Governor as commander-in-chief of state armed forces.
He or she shall be commander-in-chief of the army and navy of this State, and of the militia, except when they shall be called into the service of the United States.

Section 9. Appointing power; recess appointments; confirmation.

He or she shall have power, unless herein otherwise provided, to appoint, by and with the consent of a majority of all the members elected to the Senate, such officers as he or she is or may be authorized by this Constitution or by law to appoint. He or she shall have power to fill all vacancies that may happen during the recess of the Senate, in offices to which he or she may appoint, except in the offices of Chancellor, Chief Justice and Judges, by granting Commissions which shall expire at the end of the next session of the Senate.

He or she shall have power to fill all vacancies that may happen in elective offices, except in the offices of Lieutenant-Governor and members of the General Assembly, by granting Commissions which shall expire when their successors shall be duly qualified. In case of vacancy in an elective office, except as aforesaid, a person shall be chosen to said office for the full term at the next general election, unless the vacancy shall happen within two months next before such election, in which case the election for said office shall be held at the second succeeding general election.

Unless herein otherwise provided, confirmation by the Senate of officers appointed by the Governor shall be required only where the salary, fees and emoluments of office shall exceed the sum of fifteen hundred dollars annually.

Section 10. Secretary of State; appointment, term, duties and compensation.

The Governor shall appoint, by and with the consent of a majority of all the members elected to the Senate, a Secretary of State, who shall hold office during the pleasure of the Governor. He or she shall keep a fair register of all the official acts and proceedings of the Governor, and shall, when required by either House of the General Assembly lay the same, and all papers, minutes and vouchers, relative thereto, before such House, and shall perform such other duties as shall be enjoined upon him or her by law. He or she shall have a compensation for his or her service to be fixed by law. The Secretary of State shall become a bona fide resident of the State within six months after his or her appointment; provided, however, that upon good cause shown, the Governor may grant an additional extension of six months. After becoming a resident of the State, the Secretary shall continuously be a resident of the State as long as he or she retains office. Failure to obtain or retain such residency shall be an automatic resignation from office.

Section 11. County officers; qualifications; members of Congress, federal employees and other officers holding dual office.
No person shall be elected or appointed to an office within a county who shall not have a right to vote for a Representative in the General Assembly, and have been a resident therein one year next before his or her election or appointment, nor hold the office longer than he or she continues to reside in the county, unless herein otherwise provided.

No member of Congress, nor any person holding or exercising any office under the United States, except officers usually appointed by the courts of justice respectively and attorneys-at-law, shall at the same time hold or exercise any office of profit under this State, unless herein otherwise provided.
No person shall hold more than one of the following offices at the same time, to-wit: Secretary of State, Attorney-General, Insurance Commissioner, State Treasurer, Auditor of Accounts, Prothonotary, Clerk of the Peace, Register of Wills, Recorder, or Sheriff.

Section 12. Commissions.
All Commissions shall be in the name of the State, and shall be sealed with the great seal and signed by the Governor.

Section 13. Removal of officers by Governor; procedure.
The Governor may for any reasonable cause remove any officer, except the Lieutenant-Governor and members of the General Assembly, upon the address of two-thirds of all the members elected to each House of the General Assembly. Whenever the General Assembly shall so address the Governor, the cause of removal shall be entered on the journals of each House. The person against whom the General Assembly may be about to proceed shall receive notice thereof, accompanied with the cause alleged for his or her removal, at least ten days before the day on which either House of the General Assembly shall act thereon.

Section 14. Reports from executive departments.
The Governor may require information in writing from the officers in the executive department, upon any subject relating to the duties of their respective offices.

Section 15. Messages to General Assembly.
He or she shall, from time to time, give to the General Assembly information of affairs concerning the State and recommend to its consideration such measures as he or she shall judge expedient.

Section 16. Special sessions of General Assembly; adjournment; special session of Senate.
He or she may on extraordinary occasions convene the General Assembly by proclamation; and in case of disagreement between the two Houses with respect to the time of adjournment, adjourn them to such time as he or she shall think proper, not exceeding three months. He or she shall have power to convene the Senate in extraordinary session by proclamation, for the transaction of executive business.

Section 17. Execution of laws.
He or she shall take care that the laws be faithfully executed.

Section 18 Approval or veto of bills, orders, resolutions or votes; repassage over veto.

Every bill which shall have passed both Houses of the General Assembly shall, before it becomes law, be presented to the Governor; if he or she approves, he or she shall sign it; but if he or she shall not approve, he or she shall return it with his or her objections to the House in which it shall have originated, which House shall enter the objections at large on the journal and proceed to reconsider it. If, after such reconsideration, three-fifths of all the members elected to that House shall agree to pass the bill, it shall be sent together with the objections to the other House, by which it shall likewise be reconsidered, and if approved by three-fifths of all the members elected to that House, it shall become a law; but in neither House shall the vote be taken on the day on which the bill shall be returned to it. In all such cases the votes of both Houses shall be determined by yeas and nays, and the names of the members voting for and against the bill shall be entered on the journal of each House respectively. If any bill shall not be returned by the Governor within ten days, Sundays excepted, after it shall have been presented to him or her, the same shall be a law in like manner as if he or she had signed it, unless the General Assembly shall, by final adjournment, prevent its return, in which case it shall not become a law without the approval of the Governor.

For purposes of return of Bills not approved by the Governor the General Assembly shall be considered to be continuously in Session until final adjournment and the Clerk of the House of Representatives and the Secretary of the Senate shall be deemed proper recipients of such returned bills during recess or adjournment of the General Assembly other than final adjournment.

No bill shall become a law after the final adjournment of the General Assembly, unless approved by the Governor within thirty days after such adjournment. The Governor shall have power to disapprove of any item or items of any bill making appropriations of money, embracing distinct items, and the part or parts of the bill approved shall be the law, and the item or items of appropriation disapproved shall be void, unless repassed according to the rules and limitations prescribed for the passage of other bills, over the Executive veto. Every order, resolution, or vote to which the concurrence of both Houses of the General Assembly may be necessary, except on a question of adjournment, shall be presented to the Governor, and before the same shall take effect be approved by him or her, or being disapproved by him or her, shall be repassed by three-fifths of all the members elected to each House of the General Assembly, according to the rules and limitations prescribed in the case of a bill. Every order and resolution to which the concurrence of both Houses of the General Assembly may be necessary, except on a question of adjournment and those matters dealing solely with the internal or administrative affairs of the General Assembly, shall be presented to the Governor, and before the same shall take effect be approved by him or her, or being disapproved by him or her, shall be repassed by three-fifths of all the members elected to each House of the General Assembly, according to the rules and limitations prescribed in the case of a bill.

Section 19. Lieutenant-Governor; election, term and qualifications; President of the Senate; compensation.
A Lieutenant-Governor shall be chosen at the same time, in the same manner, for the same term, and subject to the same provisions as the Governor; he or she shall possess the same qualifications of eligibility for office as the Governor; he or she shall be President of the Senate, but shall have no vote unless the Senate be equally divided.

The Lieutenant-Governor, for his or her services as President of the Senate, shall receive the same compensation as the Speaker of the House of Representatives; the Lieutenant-Governor, for his or her services as a member of the Board of Pardons and for all other duties of the said office which may be provided by law, shall receive such compensation as shall be fixed by the General Assembly.

Section 20. Vacancy in offices of both Governor and Lieutenant-Governor; officers eligible to act; disability of Governor.

(a) In case the person elected Governor shall die or become disqualified before the commencement of his or her term of office, or shall refuse to take the same, or in case of the removal of the Governor from office, or of his or her death, resignation, or inability to discharge the powers and duties of the said office, the same shall devolve on the Lieutenant-Governor; and in case of removal, death, resignation, or inability of both the Governor and Lieutenant-Governor, the Secretary of State, or if there be none, or in case of his or her removal, death, resignation, or inability, then the Attorney-General, or if there be none, or in case of his or her removal, death, resignation, or inability, then the President pro tempore of the Senate or if there be none, or in case of his or her removal, death, resignation, or inability, then the Speaker of the House of Representatives shall act as Governor until the disability of the Governor or Lieutenant-Governor is removed, or a Governor shall be duly elected and qualified.

The foregoing provisions of this section shall apply only to such persons as are eligible to the office of Governor under this Constitution at the time the powers and duties of the office of Governor shall devolve upon them respectively.
Whenever the powers and duties of the office of Governor shall devolve upon the Lieutenant-Governor, Secretary of State, or Attorney-General, his or her office shall become vacant; and whenever the powers and duties of the office of Governor shall devolve upon the President pro tempore of the Senate, or the Speaker of the House of Representatives, his or her seat as a member of the General Assembly shall become vacant; and any such vacancy shall be filled as directed by this Constitution; provided, however, that such vacancy shall not be created in case either of the said persons shall be acting as Governor during a temporary disability of the Governor.

(b) Whenever the Governor transmits to the President pro tempore of the Senate and the Speaker of the House of Representatives his or her written declaration that he or she is unable to discharge the powers and duties of his or her office, and until he or she transmits to them a written declaration to the contrary, such powers and duties shall be discharged by the Lieutenant Governor as Acting Governor.

Whenever the Chief Justice of the Delaware Supreme Court, the President of the Medical Society of Delaware and the Commissioner of the Department of Mental Health, acting unanimously, transmit to the President pro tempore of the Senate and the Speaker of the House of Representatives, their written declaration that the Governor is unable to discharge the powers and duties of his or her office because of mental or physical disability, the Lieutenant Governor shall immediately assume the powers and duties of the office as Acting Governor. Thereafter, when the Governor transmits to the President pro tempore of the Senate and the Speaker of the House of Representatives his or her written declaration that no disability exists, he or she shall resume the powers and duties of his or her office unless the Chief Justice of the Supreme Court of Delaware, the President of the Medical Society of Delaware and the Commissioner of the Department of Mental Health, acting unanimously, transmit within five days to the President pro tempore of the Senate and the Speaker of the House of Representatives their written declaration that the Governor is unable to discharge the powers and duties of his or her office because of mental or physical disability. Thereupon the General Assembly shall decide the issue, assembling within seventy-two hours for that purpose if not then in session. If the General Assembly within ten days after receipt of the latter written declaration determines by two-thirds vote of all the members elected to each house that the Governor is unable to discharge the powers and duties of his or her office because of mental or physical disability, the Lieutenant Governor shall continue to discharge same as Acting Governor; otherwise, the Governor shall resume the powers and duties of his or her office.

Section 21. Election and term of office for certain state officers.

The terms of the Office of the Attorney General, the Insurance Commissioner, the Auditor of Accounts and the State Treasurer shall be 4 years. These officers shall be chosen by the qualified electors of the State at general elections, and be commissioned by the Governor.

Section 22. Election and term of office of certain county officers; commission.

The terms of office of Clerks of the Peace, Registers of Wills, Recorders, and Sheriffs shall be 4 years. These officers shall be chosen by the qualified electors of the respective counties at general elections, and be commissioned by the Governor.

Section 23. Place of office of certain county officers.

Prothonotaries, Clerks of the Peace, Registers of Wills, Recorders and Sheriffs shall keep their offices in the town or place in each county in which the Superior Court is usually held.

Section 24. Abolition of office of Clerk of Orphans Court; transfer of functions.

Repealed.

ARTICLE IV: JUDICIARY

Section 1. Creation of courts.
The judicial power of this State shall be vested in a Supreme Court, a Superior Court, a Court of Chancery, a Family Court, a Court of Common Pleas, a Register's Court, Justices of the Peace, and such other courts as the General Assembly, with the concurrence of two-thirds of all the Members elected to each House, shall have by law established prior to the time this amended Article IV of this Constitution becomes effective or shall from time to time by law establish after such time.

Section 2. Justices of Supreme Court and other State Judges; qualifications; residence; precedence.
There shall be five Justices of the Supreme Court who shall be citizens of the State and learned in the law. One of them shall be the Chief Justice who shall be designated as such by his or her appointment and who when present shall preside at all sittings of the Court. In the absence of the Chief Justice the Justice present who is senior in length of service shall preside. If it is otherwise impossible to determine seniority among the Justices, they shall determine it by lot and certify accordingly to the Governor.
In addition to members of the Supreme Court there shall be other State Judges, who shall be citizens of the State and learned in the law. They shall include: (1) the Chancellor and the Vice-Chancellors; (2) The President Judge and the Judges of the Superior Court, three of whom shall be Resident Associate Judges and one of whom shall after appointment reside in each county of the State; (3) the Chief Judge and the Judges of the Family Court; (4) the Chief Judge and Judges of the Court of Common Pleas, one of whom after appointment shall reside in each county of the State; and (5) the Chief Magistrate of the Justice of the Peace Court.

There shall also be such number of additional Vice-Chancellors and Judges as may hereinafter be provided for by Act of the General Assembly. Each of such Vice-Chancellors and Judges shall be citizens of the State and learned in the law.

If it is otherwise impossible to determine seniority of service among the Vice-Chancellors or among the said Judges, they shall determine it by lot respectively and certify accordingly to the Governor.

The tenure and status of the Justices of the Supreme Court and State Judges as shall have been appointed as provided for by the Constitution or by Act of the General Assembly prior to the time this amended Article IV of this Constitution becomes effective shall in no wise be affected.

Section 3. Appointment of judges; terms of office; vacancies; political representation; confirmation of appointment.

The Chief Justice and Justices of the Supreme Court, the Chancellor and Vice-Chancellors of the Court of Chancery, the President Judge and Judges of the Superior Court, the Chief Judge and Judges of the Family Court, the Chief Judge and Judges of the Court of Common Pleas, and the Chief Magistrate of the Justice of the Peace Court shall be appointed by the Governor, by and with the consent of a majority of all the members elected to the Senate, for a term of 12 years each, and the persons so appointed shall enter upon the discharge of the duties of their respective offices upon taking the oath of office prescribed by this Constitution. The Governor shall submit his or her appointment within a period from 30 days before to 90 days after the occurrence of a vacancy howsoever caused. If a vacancy shall occur, by expiration of term or otherwise, at a time when the Senate shall not be in session, the Governor shall within a period from 30 days before to 90 days after the happening of any such vacancy convene the Senate for the purpose of confirming his or her appointment to fill said vacancy and the transaction of such other executive business as may come before it. Such vacancy shall be filled as aforesaid for the full term. Notwithstanding a vacancy, whether occurring when the Senate is or is not in session, an incumbent whose term has expired may hold over in office until the incumbent, or a new appointee, is confirmed and takes the oath of office for the next term, but in no event shall an incumbent whose term has expired hold over in office for more than 90 days after the expiration of the term. In all instances, the term of a new or reappointed Chief Justice or Justice of the Supreme Court, Chancellor or Vice-Chancellor of the Court of Chancery, President Judge or Judge of the Superior Court, the Chief Judge and Judges of the Family Court, the Chief Judge and Judges of the Court of Common Pleas, or Chief Magistrate of the Justice of the Peace Court shall begin after the occurrence of the vacancy and on the date the oath of office is taken, thus qualifying the individual to serve, but the appointment shall be forfeited if such oath is not taken within 30 days of confirmation.

Appointments to the office of the State Judiciary shall at all times be subject to all of the following limitations:

First, three of the five Justices of the Supreme Court in office at the same time, shall be of one major political party, and two of said Justices shall be of the other major political party.

Second, at any time when the total number of Judges of the Superior Court shall be an even number not more than one-half of the members of all such offices shall be of the same political party; and at any time when the number of such offices shall be an odd number, then not more than a bare majority of the members of all such offices shall be of the same major political party, the remaining members of such offices shall be of the other major political party.

Third, at any time when the total number of the offices of the Justices of the Supreme Court, the Judges of the Superior Court, the Chancellor and all the Vice-Chancellors shall be an even number, not more than one-half of the members of all such offices shall be of the same major political party; and at any time when the total number of such offices shall be an odd number, then not more than a bare majority of the members of all such offices shall be of the same major political party; the remaining members of the Courts above enumerated shall be of the other major political party.

Fourth, at any time when the total number of Judges of the Family Court shall be an even number, not more than one-half of the Judges shall be of the same political party; and at any time when the total number of Judges shall be an odd number, then not more than a majority of one Judge shall be of the same political party.

Fifth, at any time when the total number of Judges of the Court of Common Pleas shall be an even number, not more than one-half of the Judges shall be of the same political party; and at any time when the total number of Judges shall be an odd number, then not more than a majority of one Judge shall be of the same political party.

Sixth, before sending the name of any person to the Senate for confirmation as the appointment of the Governor to a vacancy in any Judicial Office as aforesaid, the Governor shall, not less than ten (10) days before sending the name of such person to the Senate for confirmation, address a public letter to the President of the Senate informing him or her that he or she intends to submit to the Senate for confirmation as an appointment to such vacancy the name of the person he or she intends to appoint.

Section 4. Compensation of judges; method of payment; receipt of other fees or holding other office.
The Justices of the Supreme Court, the Chancellor and the Vice-Chancellor or Vice-Chancellors, the President Judge and Judges of the Superior Court, the Chief Judge and Judges of the Family Court, the Chief Judge and Judges of the Court of Common Pleas and the Chief Magistrate of the Justice of the Peace Court shall respectively receive from the State for their services compensations which shall be fixed by law and paid monthly and they shall not receive any fees or perquisites in addition to their salaries for business done by them except as provided by law. They shall hold no other office of profit.

Section 5. Composition of Superior Court; presiding judge; quorum.

The President Judge of the Superior Court and the Judges thereof shall compose the Superior Court, as hereinafter prescribed. In each of the said courts the President Judge when present shall preside, and in his or her absence the senior Judge present shall preside.

One Judge shall constitute a quorum of the said courts, respectively, except in the Superior Court sitting to try cases of prosecution under Section 8 of Article V of this Constitution, when two Judges shall constitute a quorum. One Judge may open and adjourn any of said courts.

Section 6. Sessions of Superior Court.

Subject to the provisions of Section 5 of this Article two or more sessions of the Superior Court may at the same time be held in the same County or in different Counties.

Section 7. Jurisdiction of Superior Court.

The Superior Court shall have jurisdiction of all causes of a civil nature, real, personal and mixed, at common law and all the other jurisdiction and powers vested by the laws of this State in the formerly existing Superior Court; and also shall have all the jurisdiction and powers vested by the laws of this State in the formerly existing Court of General Sessions of the Peace and Jail Delivery; and also shall have all the jurisdiction and powers vested by the laws of this State in the formerly existing Court of General Sessions; and also shall have all the jurisdiction and powers vested by the laws of this State in the formerly existing Court of Oyer and Terminer.

Section 7A. Jurisdiction of Family Court.

The Family court shall have all the jurisdiction and powers vested by the laws of this State in the Family Court.

Section 7B. Jurisdiction of Court of Common Pleas.

The Court of Common Pleas shall have all the jurisdiction and powers vested by the laws of this State in the Court of Common Pleas.

Section 8. Definitions of particular terms.

The phrase "Supreme Court" as used in Section 4 of Article V of this Constitution and the phrases "Superior Court," "Court of General Sessions of the Peace and Jail Delivery," "Court of Oyer and Terminer" and "Court of General Sessions" wherever found in the law of this State, elsewhere than in this amended Article IV of this Constitution, shall be read as and taken to mean, and hereafter printed as, the Superior Court provided for in this amended Article IV of this Constitution; and the phrase "Chief Justice" wherever found in the law of this State existing at the time this amended Article IV of this Constitution becomes effective, elsewhere than in this amended Article IV of this Constitution, shall be read as and taken to mean, and hereafter printed as President Judge of the Superior Court, as provided for in this amended Article IV of this Constitution.

Section 9. Jurisdiction of Orphans Court.

Repealed.

Section 10. Composition and jurisdiction of Court of Chancery; initiation and decisions in causes and proceedings.

The Chancellor and the Vice-Chancellor or Vice-Chancellors shall hold the Court of Chancery. One of them, respectively, shall sit alone in that court. This court shall have all the jurisdiction and powers vested by the laws of this State in the Court of Chancery. In any cause or matter in the Court of Chancery that is initiated by an application to a Judge of that Court, the application may be made directly to the Chancellor or a Vice-Chancellor. Causes or proceedings in the Court of Chancery shall be decided, and orders or decrees therein shall be made by the Chancellor or Vice-Chancellor who hears them, respectively.

Section 11. Jurisdiction of Supreme Court.
The Supreme Court shall have jurisdiction as follows:

(1)(a) To receive appeals from the Superior Court in civil causes and to determine finally all matters of appeal in the interlocutory or final judgments and other proceedings of said Superior Court in civil causes: Provided that on appeal from a verdict of a jury, the findings of the jury, if supported by evidence, shall be conclusive.

(1)(b) To receive appeals from the Superior Court in criminal causes, upon application of the accused in all cases in which the sentence shall be death, imprisonment exceeding one month, or fine exceeding One Hundred Dollars, and in such other cases as shall be provided by law; and to determine finally all matters of appeal on the judgments and proceedings of said Superior Court in criminal causes: Provided, however, that appeals from the Superior Court in cases of prosecution under Section 8 of Article V of this Constitution shall be governed by the provisions of that Section.

(1)(c) Notwithstanding any provisions of this Section to the contrary, to receive appeals from the Superior Court in criminal causes, upon application by the State in all causes in which the Superior Court, or any inferior court an appeal from which lies to the Superior Court, has granted an accused any of the following: a new trial or judgment of acquittal after a verdict, modification of a verdict, arrest of judgment, relief in any post-conviction proceeding or in any action collaterally attacking a criminal judgment, or a new punishment hearing in a capital case after the court has imposed a sentence of death, or any order or judgment declaring any act of the General Assembly, or any portion of any such act, to be unconstitutional under either the Constitution of the United States or the State of Delaware, inoperative or unenforceable, except that no appeal shall lie where otherwise prohibited by the double jeopardy clause of the Constitution of the United States or of this State.

Notwithstanding anything in this Article to the contrary, the General Assembly may by statute implement the jurisdiction herein conferred.

(2) Wherever in this Constitution reference is made to a writ of error or a proceeding in error to the Superior Court, such reference shall be construed as referring to the appeal provided for in Section (1)(a) and Section (1)(b) of this Article.

(3) To receive appeals from the Superior Court in cases of prosecution under Section 8 of Article V of this Constitution and to determine finally all matters of appeal in such cases.

(4) To receive appeals from the Court of Chancery and to determine finally all matters of appeal in the interlocutory or final decrees and other proceedings in chancery.

(5) To issue writs of prohibition, quo warranto, certiorari and mandamus to the Superior Court, and the Court of Chancery; or any of the Judges of the said courts and also to any inferior court or courts established or to be established by law and to any of the Judges thereof and to issue all orders, rules and processes proper to give effect to the same. The General Assembly shall have power to provide by law in what manner the jurisdiction and power hereby conferred may be exercised in vacation and whether by one or more Justices of the Supreme Court.

(6) To issue such temporary writs or orders in causes pending on appeal, or on writ of error, as may be necessary to protect the rights of parties and any Justice of the Supreme Court may exercise this power when the court is not in session.

(7) To exercise such other jurisdiction by way of appeal, writ of error or of certiorari as the General Assembly may from time to time confer upon it.

(8) To hear and determine questions of law certified to it by other Delaware courts, the Supreme Court of the United States, a Court of Appeals of the United States, a United States District Court, a United States Bankruptcy Court, the United States Securities and Exchange Commission, the highest appellate court of any other state, the highest appellate court of any foreign country, or any foreign governmental agency regulating the public issuance or trading of securities, where it appears to the Supreme Court that there are important and urgent reasons for an immediate determination of such questions by it. The Supreme Court may, by rules, define generally the conditions under which questions may be certified to it and prescribe methods of certification.

Section 12. Composition of Supreme Court; designation of temporary Justices; quorum; opening and adjourning court.

A quorum of the Supreme Court shall consist of not less than three Justices. The entire Court shall sit in any criminal case in which the accused has been sentenced to death and in such other civil and criminal cases as the Court, by rule, or the General Assembly, upon the concurrence of two-thirds of all the members elected to each house, shall determine. In case of a lack of quorum by reason of vacancies in their number, incapacity, or disqualification to sit by reason of interest, or to constitute a three-member panel of the Court, the Chief Justice of the Supreme Court, or in case of his or her absence from the State, disqualification, incapacity, or if there be a vacancy in that office, the next qualified and available Justice, who by seniority is next in rank to the Chief Justice, shall have the power to designate judges from among the judges of the constitutional courts to sit in the Supreme Court temporarily to satisfy the number of Justices required by law. It shall be the duty of the judges of the constitutional courts so designated to sit accordingly. No judge shall be so designated to sit in the Supreme Court in any cause in which he or she sat below. Any one of the Justices of the Supreme Court may open and adjourn court.

Section 13. Administrative head of courts; supervisory powers; designation of judges to sit in Court of Chancery, or the Superior Court.

The Chief Justice of the Supreme Court, or in case of his or her absence from the State, disqualification, incapacity, or if there be a vacancy in that office, the next qualified and available Justice who by seniority is next in rank to the Chief Justice shall be administrative head of all the courts in the State, and shall have general administrative and supervisory powers over all the courts. Such powers shall include but shall not be limited to the following:

(1) Upon the approval of a majority of the Justices of the Supreme Court to adopt rules for the administration of justice and the conduct of the business of any or all the courts in this State: Provided, however, that any other of the courts in this State may from time to time, subject to the exercise of the power in this paragraph (1) conferred upon the Justices of the Supreme Court, adopt rules of pleading practice and procedure applicable to such Court.

(2) Upon written request made by the Chancellor, President Judge of the Superior Court, the Chief Judge of the Family Court, or the Chief Judge of the Court of Common Pleas, or in the event of an absence or incapacity, by the next qualified and available Vice-Chancellor, or Judge, who is senior in length of service, to designate one or more of the State Judges (including the Justices of the Supreme Court) to sit in the Court of Chancery, the Superior Court, the Family Court or the Court of Common Pleas, as the case may be, and to hear and decide such causes in such Court and for such period of time as shall be designated. It shall be the duty of the State Judge so designated to serve according to such designation as a Judge of the Court designated. The provisions of this paragraph shall not be deemed to limit in any manner the powers conferred upon the judges of the Superior Court under Section 14 of this Article.

Section 14. Power of law judges to grant restraining orders and preliminary injunctions.

The President Judge of the Superior Court or any Judge shall have power, in the absence of the Chancellor and all the Vice-Chancellors from the county where any suit in equity may be instituted or during the temporary disability of the Chancellor and all the Vice-Chancellors, to grant restraining orders, and the said President Judge or any Judge shall have power, during the absence of the Chancellor and all the Vice-Chancellors from the State or his or her and their temporary disability, to grant preliminary injunctions pursuant to the rules and practice of the Court of Chancery; provided that nothing herein contained shall be construed to confer general jurisdiction over the case.

Section 15. Judges ad litem; limitation and expiration of commission; compensation; persons not disqualified.
The Governor shall have power to commission a judge or judges ad litem to sit in any cause in any of said Courts when by reason of legal exception to the Judges authorized to sit therein, or for other cause, there are not a sufficient number of Judges available to hold such Court. The commission in such case shall confine the office to the cause and it shall expire on the determination of the cause. The judge so appointed shall receive reasonable compensation to be fixed by the General Assembly. A Member of Congress, or any person holding or exercising an office under the United States, shall not be disqualified from being appointed a judge ad litem.

Section 16. Scope of jurisdiction and process; costs.
The jurisdiction of each of the aforesaid courts shall be coextensive with the State. Process may be issued out of each court, in any county, into every county. No costs shall be awarded against any party to a cause by reason of the fact that suit is brought in a county other than that in which the defendant or defendants may reside at the time of bringing suit.

Section 17. Jurisdictional changes by General Assembly; appeals to Supreme Court.
The General Assembly, notwithstanding anything contained in this Article, shall have power to repeal or alter any Act of the General Assembly giving jurisdiction to the former Court of Oyer and Terminer, the former Superior Court, the former Court of General Sessions of the Peace and Jail Delivery, the former Court of General Sessions, the Superior Court hereby established, the Family Court hereby established, the Court of Common Pleas hereby established or the Court of Chancery, in any matter, or giving any power to any of the said courts. The General Assembly shall also have power to confer upon the Superior

Court, the Family Court, the Court of Common Pleas and the Court of Chancery jurisdiction and powers in addition to those hereinbefore mentioned. Until the General Assembly shall otherwise direct, there shall be an appeal to the Supreme Court in all cases in which there is an appeal, according to any Act of the General Assembly, to the former Court of Errors and Appeals or to the former Supreme Court of this State.

Section 18. Powers of Chancellor, Vice-Chancellors and Judges.

Until the General Assembly shall otherwise provide, the Chancellor and the Vice-Chancellor or Vice-Chancellors, respectively, shall exercise all the powers which any law of this State vests in the Chancellor, besides the general powers of the Court of Chancery, and the President Judge of the Superior Court and the Judges of said Courts shall each singly exercise all the powers which any law of this State vests in the Judges singly of the former Superior Court, whether as members of the Court or otherwise.

Until the General Assembly shall otherwise provide, the Chief Judge of the Family Court and the Judges of said Court, respectively, shall each singly exercise all the powers which any law of this State vests in the Judges of Family Court, whether as members of the Court or otherwise, and the Chief Judge of the Court of Common Pleas and the Judges of said Court, respectively, shall each singly exercise all the powers which any law of the State vests in the Judges of the Court of Common Pleas, whether as members of the Court or otherwise.

Section 19. Instructions to jury.

Judges shall not charge juries with respect to matters of fact, but may state the questions of fact in issue and declare the law.

Section 20. Trial by court of issues of fact in civil causes.

In civil causes where matters of fact are at issue, if the parties agree, such matters of fact shall be tried by the court, and judgment rendered upon their decision thereon as upon a verdict by a jury.

Section 21. Amendments in civil pleadings and proceedings by Superior Court; examination of witnesses and parties.

In civil causes, when pending, the Superior Court shall have the power, before judgment, of directing, upon such terms as it shall deem reasonable, amendments in pleadings and legal proceedings, so that by error in any of them, the determination of causes, according to their real merits, shall not be hindered; and also of directing the examination of witnesses and parties litigant.

Section 22. Payment into court pending action for debt or damages; costs.

At any time pending an action for debt or damages, the defendant may bring into court a sum of money for discharging the same, together with the costs then accrued and the plaintiff not accepting the same, if upon the final decision of the cause, he or she shall not recover a greater sum than that so paid into court for him or her, he or she shall not recover any costs accruing after such payment, except where the plaintiff is an executor or administrator.

Section 23. Survival of action; executor or administrator as party; continuance.

By the death of any party, no suit in chancery or at law, where the cause of action survives, shall abate, but, until the General Assembly shall otherwise provide, suggestion of such death being entered of record, the executor or administrator of a deceased petitioner or plaintiff may prosecute the said suit; and if a respondent or defendant dies, the executor or administrator being duly serviced with a scire facias thirty (30) days before the return thereof shall be considered as a party to the suit, in the same manner as if he or she had voluntarily made himself or herself a party; and in any of those cases, the court shall pass a decree, or render judgment for or against executors or administrators as to right appertains. But where an executor or administrator of a deceased respondent or defendant becomes a party, the court upon motion shall grant such a continuance of the cause as to the judges shall appear proper.

Section 24. Security for stay of proceedings on appeal or writ of error.

Whenever a person, not being an executor or administrator, appeals or applies to the Supreme Court for a writ of error, such appeal or writ shall be no stay of proceedings in the court below unless the appellant or plaintiff in error shall give sufficient security to be approved by the court below or by a judge of the Supreme Court that the appellant or plaintiff in error shall prosecute respectively his or her appeal or writ to effect, and pay the condemnation money and all costs, or otherwise abide the decree in appeal or the judgment in error, if he or she fail to make his or her plea good.

Section 25. Chief Register in Chancery: appointment; powers and duties.

The Court of Chancery shall appoint a Chief Register in Chancery to hold office at the pleasure of that Court. The Chief Register in Chancery shall be the Clerk of the Court of Chancery and shall appoint, with the concurrence of the Court, a Register in Chancery in each county who shall also serve at the pleasure of Court. The Chief Register in Chancery may also appoint other deputies, issue process, and enter judgment and do such other things as are according to law and the practice of the court.

Section 26. Prothonotary as Clerk of Superior Court; powers and duties; entry of testatum fieri facias.

The Superior Court shall appoint a Prothonotary in each county to hold office at the pleasure of the said Court. The Prothonotary of each County shall be the Clerk of the Superior Court in and for the County in which he or she holds office. He or she may issue process, take recognizance of bail and enter judgments, according to law and the practice of the court. No judgment in one county shall bind lands or tenements in another until a testatum fieri facias being issued shall be entered of record in the office of the Prothonotary of the County wherein the lands or tenements are situated. Such Prothonotary shall perform all duties heretofore performed by the Clerk of the Peace as Clerk of the former Court of General Sessions and the former Court of Oyer and Terminer. This section shall not be interpreted to prevent the transfer of a judgment from any court of one county to the Superior Court of another county pursuant to legislation enacted by the General Assembly, nor shall it be construed to require the issuance or entry into the record of a testatum fieri facias when a judgment is transferred from a court of one county to the Superior Court of another county pursuant to legislation enacted by the General Assembly.

Section 27. Clerk of Supreme Court; term of office and compensation.

The Supreme Court shall have the power to appoint a Clerk to hold office at the pleasure of the said Court. He or she shall receive from the State for his or her services a compensation which shall be fixed from time to time by the said Court and paid monthly.

Section 28. Criminal jurisdiction of inferior courts and justices of the peace; regulation of jurisdiction; indictment; jury trial; appeals.

The General Assembly may by law give to any inferior courts by it established or to be established, or to one or more justices of the peace, jurisdiction of the criminal matters following, that is to say -- assaults and batteries, carrying concealed a deadly weapon, disturbing meetings held for the purpose of religious worship, nuisances, and such other misdemeanors as the General Assembly may from time to time, with the concurrence of two-thirds of all the Members elected to each House, prescribe.

The General Assembly may by law regulate this jurisdiction, and provide that the proceedings shall be with or without indictment by grand jury, or trial by petit jury, and may grant or deny the privilege of appeal to the Superior Court; provided, however, that there shall be an appeal to the Superior Court in all cases in which the sentence shall be imprisonment exceeding one (1) month, or a fine exceeding One Hundred Dollars ($100.00).

Section 29. Justices of the Peace; term of office; powers of the Chief Magistrate and Justices of the Peace.

There shall be appointed, as hereinafter provided, such number of persons to the Office of Justice of the Peace as directed by law, who shall be commissioned as follows:

(a) Upon first appointment and confirmation, a Justice of the Peace shall be commissioned for four (4) years:
(b) Upon second or third appointment and confirmation, a Justice of the Peace shall be commissioned for six (6) years:
(c) Upon fourth or subsequent appointments and confirmation, a Justice of the Peace shall be commissioned for eight (8) years.

Section 30. Justices of the Peace, Chief Magistrate, and judges of legislative courts; appointment by Governor; terms of office.

Justices of the Peace and the judges of such courts as the General Assembly may establish, or shall have established prior to the time this amended Article IV of this Constitution becomes effective, pursuant to the provisions of Section 1 or Section 28 of this Article, shall be appointed by the Governor, by and with the consent of a majority of all the Members elected to the Senate, for such terms as shall be fixed by this Constitution or by law. The Chief Magistrate shall be appointed and confirmed subject to the provisions of Section 3 of this Article.

Section 31. Registers of Wills; depositions of witnesses; process; appeals to Court of Chancery; disqualification of Register for interest.

The Registers of Wills of the several counties shall respectively hold the Register's Court in each County. Upon the litigation of a cause the depositions of the witnesses examined shall be taken at large in writing and made part of the proceedings in the cause. This court may issue process throughout the State.

Appeals may be taken from a Register's Court to the Court of Chancery. In cases where a Register of Wills is interested in questions concerning the probate of wills, the granting of letters of administration, or executors' or administrators' accounts, the cognizance thereof shall belong to the Court of Chancery.

Section 32. Adjustment and settlement of executors' and administrators' accounts; notice; hearing of exceptions in Court of Chancery; transfer of jurisdiction; appeals.
An executor or administrator shall file every account with the Register of Wills for the County, who shall, as soon as conveniently may be, carefully examine the particulars with the proofs thereof, in the presence of such executor or administrator, and shall adjust and settle the same according to the right of the matter and the law of the land; which account so settled shall remain in his or her office for inspection; and the executor, or administrator, shall within three (3) months after such settlement give notice in writing to all persons entitled to shares of the estate, or to their guardians, respectively, if residing within the State, that the account is lodged in the said office for inspection. Exceptions may be made by persons concerned to both sides of every such account, either denying the justice of the allowances made to the accountant or alleging further charges against him or her; and the exceptions shall be heard in the Court of Chancery for the County; and thereupon the account shall be adjusted and settled according to the right of the matter and the law of the land.

The General Assembly shall have power to transfer to the Court of Chancery all or a part of the jurisdiction by this Constitution vested in the Register of Wills and to vest in the Court of Chancery all or a part of such jurisdiction and to provide for appeals from that Court exercising such jurisdiction.

Section 33. Style of process and public acts; prosecutions in name of State.

The style in all process and public acts shall be THE STATE OF DELAWARE. Prosecutions shall be carried on in the name of the State.

Section 34. Continuation in office and designation of certain judicial officers.

The Chancellor, Chief Justice and Judges in office at and immediately before the time this amended Article IV of this Constitution becomes effective shall hold their respective offices until the expiration of their terms respectively and shall receive the compensation provided by law. They shall, however, be hereafter designated as follows:

The Chancellor shall continue to be designated as Chancellor; The Chief Justice shall hereafter be designated as President Judge of the Superior Court;

The Judges shall hereafter be designated as Judges of the Superior Court.

The Vice-Chancellor in office at and immediately before the time this amended Article IV of this Constitution becomes effective shall hold his or her office until the expiration of the period of twelve years from the date of the commission for the office of Vice-Chancellor held by him or her at the time this amended Article IV of this Constitution becomes effective and shall receive the compensation provided by law. He or she shall continue to be designated as Vice-Chancellor.

Section 34A. Continuation in office and designation of judicial officers of the Family Court and the Court of Common Pleas.

The Chief Judge and the Judges of the Family Court and the Chief Judge and the Judges of the Court of Common Pleas in office at and immediately before the time this amended Article IV of this Constitution becomes effective shall hold their respective offices until the expiration of their terms, respectively, and shall receive the compensation provided by law.

Section 35. Proceedings pending at time of 1951 amendment; books, records and papers; effect of amended article on Court of Chancery.

All writs of error and appeals and proceedings pending, at the time this amended Article IV of this Constitution becomes effective, in the Supreme Court as heretofore constituted shall be proceeded within the Supreme Court hereby established, and all the books, records and papers of the said Supreme Court as heretofore constituted shall be the books, records and papers of the Supreme Court hereby established.

All suits, proceedings and matters pending, at the time this amended Article IV of this Constitution becomes effective, in the Superior Court as heretofore constituted shall be proceeded within the Superior Court hereby established and all the books, records and papers of the said Superior Court as heretofore constituted shall be the books, records and papers of the Superior Court hereby established.

All indictments, proceedings and matters of a criminal nature pending in the former Court of General Sessions and in the former Court of Oyer and Terminer, at the time this amended Article IV of this Constitution becomes effective, and all books, records and papers of said former Court of General Sessions and former Court of Oyer and Terminer shall be transferred to the Superior Court hereby established, and the said indictments, proceedings and matters pending shall be proceeded with to final judgment and determination in the said Superior Court hereby established.

The Court of Chancery is not affected by this amended Article IV of this Constitution otherwise than by the provisions with respect to a Vice-Chancellor or Vice-Chancellors.

Section 36. Abolition of Orphans Court; transfer of jurisdiction and powers.

Repealed.

Section 37. Court on the Judiciary.
A Court on the Judiciary is hereby created consisting of the Chief Justice and the Justices of the Supreme Court, the Chancellor, the President Judge of the Superior Court, the Chief Judge of the Family Court, the Chief Judge of the Court of Common Pleas and the Chief Magistrate of the Justice of the Peace Court.
Any judicial officer appointed by the Governor may be censured or removed or retired by the Court on the Judiciary as herein provided.

A judicial officer may be censured or removed by virtue of this section for wilful misconduct in office, wilful and persistent failure to perform his or her duties, the commission after appointment of an offense involving moral turpitude, or other persistent misconduct in violation of the Canons of Judicial Ethics as adopted by the Delaware Supreme Court from time to time.
A judicial officer may be retired by virtue of this section for permanent mental or physical disability interfering with the proper performance of the duties of his or her office.
No judicial officer shall be censured or removed or retired under this section unless he or she has been served with a written statement of the charges against him or her, or of the grounds of his or her retirement, and shall have had an opportunity to be heard in accordance with due process of law. The affirmative concurrence of not less than two-thirds of the members of the Court on the Judiciary shall be necessary for the censure or removal or retirement of a judicial officer. The Court on the Judiciary shall be convened for appropriate action upon the order of the Chief Justice, or upon the order of any other three members of the Court on the Judiciary. All hearings and other proceedings of the Court on the Judiciary shall be private, and all records except a final order of removal or retirement shall be confidential, unless the judicial officer involved shall otherwise

request.

Upon an order of removal, the judicial officer shall thereby be removed from office, all of his or her authority, rights and privileges as a judicial officer shall cease from the date of the order, and a vacancy shall be deemed to exist as of that date. Upon an order of retirement, the judicial officer shall thereby be retired with such rights and privileges as may be provided by law for the disability retirement of a judicial officer, and a vacancy shall be deemed to exist as of the date of retirement.

In the absence or disqualification of a member of the Court on the Judiciary, the Chief Justice, or in his or her absence or disqualification the Senior Associate Justice, shall appoint a substitute member pro tempore.

The Court on the Judiciary shall have:

(a) the power to summon witnesses to appear and testify under oath and to compel the production of books, papers and documents, and
(b) the power to adopt rules establishing procedures for the investigation and trial of a judicial officer hereunder.

Section 38. Retired Judges and Justices; temporary assignment.

A former State Judge or a former Justice of the Supreme Court, who is retired and is receiving a state judicial pension and who assents to active judicial duty and who is not engaged in the practice of law, upon designation of the Chief Justice of the Supreme Court, or in case of his or her absence from the State, disqualification, incapacity, or if there be a vacancy in that office, upon designation of the next qualified and available Justice, who by seniority is next in rank to the Chief Justice, shall be authorized to sit temporarily in the court from which he or she retired or in any other court to which he or she could be designated under the Constitution and statutes of the State if he or she still held the judicial position from which he or she retired.

Any person so designated shall receive compensation as the General Assembly shall provide. Nothing herein shall authorize the designation of any former State Judge or a former Justice of the Supreme Court to sit in the Supreme Court except temporarily to fill up the number of that Court to the required quorum. The term "State Judge" as used in this section means a Chancellor or Vice-Chancellor of the Chancery Court or a President Judge or Judge of the Superior Court.

Section 39. Senior judges.
The office of Senior Judge is hereby created. Any retired judge of a court established by this amended Article IV of this Constitution or by act of the General Assembly, who is duly qualified and appointed, may serve as a Senior Judge. The qualifications, manner of appointment, term of office, compensation, duties, and all other matters relating to the office of the Senior Judge shall be as specified by statute.

Senior Judges are subject to the Code of Judicial Conduct and are subject to censure, removal or retirement by the Court on the Judiciary in accordance with Section 37 of this Article IV. Senior Judges shall not be counted for purposes of determining the political representation on any court or on any combination of courts under Section 3 of this Article IV.

ARTICLE V: ELECTIONS

Section 1. Time and manner of holding general election.

The general election shall be held biennially on the Tuesday next after the first Monday in the month of November, and shall be by ballot; but the General Assembly may by law prescribe the means, methods and instruments of voting so as best to secure secrecy and the independence of the voter, preserve the freedom and purity of elections and prevent fraud, corruption and intimidation thereat.

Section 2. Qualifications for voting; members of the Armed Services of the United States stationed within State; persons disqualified; forfeiture of right.

Every citizen of this State of the age of twenty-one years who shall have been a resident thereof one year next preceding an election, and for the last three months a resident of the county, and for the last thirty days a resident of the hundred or election district in which he or she may offer to vote, and in which he or she shall have been duly registered as hereinafter provided for, shall be entitled to vote at such election in the hundred or election district of which he or she shall at the time be a resident, and in which he or she shall be registered, for all officers that now are or hereafter may be elected by the people and upon all questions which may be submitted to the vote of the people; provided, however, that no person who shall attain the age of twenty-one years after the first day of January in the year of our Lord, nineteen hundred, or after that date shall become a citizen of the United States, shall have the right to vote unless he or she shall be able to read this Constitution in the English language and write his or her name; but these requirements shall not apply to any person who by reason of physical disability shall be unable to comply therewith; and provided also, that no person in the military, naval, or marine service of the United States shall be considered as acquiring a residence in this State, by being stationed in any garrison, barrack, or military or naval place or station within this State; and no person adjudged mentally incompetent or person convicted of a crime deemed by law felony, or incapacitated under the provisions of this Constitution from voting, shall enjoy the right of an elector; and the General Assembly may impose the forfeiture of the right of suffrage as a punishment for crime. Any person who is disqualified as a voter because of a conviction of a crime deemed by law a felony shall have such disqualification removed upon being pardoned, or after the expiration of the sentence, whichever may first occur. The term "sentence" as used in this Section shall include all periods of modification of a sentence, such as, but not limited to, probation, parole and suspension. The provision of this paragraph shall not apply to (1) those persons who were convicted of any felony of murder or manslaughter, (except vehicular homicide); or (2) those persons who were convicted of any felony constituting an offense against public administration involving bribery or improper influence or abuse of office, or any like offense under the laws of any state or local jurisdiction, or of the United States, or of the District of Columbia; or (3) those persons who were convicted of any felony constituting a sexual offense, or any like offense under the laws of any state or local jurisdiction or of the United States or of the District of Columbia.

Section 2A. Residence requirements in case of intrastate removal; election of President and Vice-President of United States; qualifications.

The General Assembly shall extend to any elector in the state who shall have changed his or her residence from one county, hundred, or election district to another, but who has not resided therein for a sufficient time so as to be eligible to vote in the county, hundred or election district to which he or she has removed, the right to vote for the choice of electors for President and Vice-President of the United States, but for no other offices, provided such citizen would have been eligible to vote within this State had he or she not moved, and provided that he or she is not entitled to vote for the choice of electors for President or Vice-President of the United States in any other place and provided further that such citizen would be an otherwise qualified voter under this Constitution except that he or she has not resided in his or her county, hundred or election district for a sufficient length of time.

Section 2B. Residence requirements of persons from other states; election of President and Vice-President of United States; qualifications.

The General Assembly shall extend to a citizen of the United States who has resided in this State for at least 3 months next preceding an election but who does not meet the residence requirements established in Article V, Section 2 of this Constitution, the right to vote for the choice of electors for President and Vice-President of the United States, but for no other offices, provided such citizen was either a qualified voter in another state immediately prior to his or her removal to this State, or would have been eligible to vote in such other state had he or she remained there until such election, and provided that he or she is not entitled to vote for the choice of electors for President or Vice-President of the United States in any other state and provided further that such citizen would be an otherwise qualified voter under this Constitution except that he or she had not resided in this State for one year.

Section 3. Influencing voter; loss of vote; challenge; oath and affirmation; perjury.

No person who shall receive or accept, or offer to receive or accept, or shall pay, transfer, or deliver, or offer or promise to pay, transfer or deliver, or shall contribute, or offer or promise to contribute to another, to be paid or used, any money or other valuable thing as a compensation, inducement or reward for the registering or abstaining from registering of any one qualified to register, or for the giving or withholding, or in any manner influencing the giving or withholding, a vote at any general or special or municipal election in this State, shall vote at such election; and upon challenge for any of said causes the person so challenged before the officers authorized for that purpose shall receive his or her vote, shall swear or affirm before such officers that he or she has not received or accepted, or offered to receive or accept, or paid, transferred or delivered, or offered or promised to pay, transfer or deliver, or contributed, or offered or promised to contribute to another, to be paid or used, any money or other valuable thing as a compensation, inducement or reward for the registering or abstaining from registering of any one qualified to register, or for the giving or withholding, or in any manner influencing the giving or withholding, a vote at such election.

Such oath or affirmation shall be conclusive evidence to the election officers of the truth of such oath or affirmation; but if any such oath or affirmation shall be false, the person making the same shall be guilty of perjury, and no conviction thereof shall bar any prosecution under Section 8 of this Article.

Section 4. Registration of voters; days for registration; application to strike name from list; appeals; registration as prerequisite for voting.
The General Assembly shall enact uniform laws for the registration of voters in this State entitled to vote under this Article, which registration shall be conclusive evidence to the election officers of the right of every person so registered to vote at any General Election while his or her name shall remain on the list of registered voters, and who is not at the time disqualified under the provisions of Section 3 of this Article; and no person shall vote at such General Election whose name does not at that time appear in said list of registered voters.

There shall be at least two registration days in a period commencing not more than one hundred and twenty days, nor less than sixty days before, and ending not more than twenty days, nor less than ten days before, each General Election, on which registration days persons whose names are not on the list of registered voters established by law for such election, may apply for registration, and on which registration days applications may be made to strike from the said registration list names of persons on said list who are not eligible to vote at such election; provided, however, that such registration may be corrected as hereinafter provided at any time prior to the day of holding the election.

From the decision of the registration officers granting or refusing registration, or striking or refusing to strike a name or names from the registration list, any person interested, or any registration officer, may appeal to the resident Associate Judge of the County, or in case of his or her disability or absence from the County, to any Judge entitled to sit in the Supreme Court, whose determination shall be final; and he or she shall have power to order any name improperly omitted from the said registry to be placed thereon, and any name improperly appearing on the said registry to be stricken therefrom, and any name appearing on the said registry, in any manner incorrect, to be corrected, and to make and enforce all necessary orders in the premises for the correction of the said registry. Registration shall be a prerequisite for voting only at general elections, at which Representatives to the General Assembly shall be chosen, unless the General Assembly shall otherwise provide by law.

The existing laws in reference to the registration of voters, so far as consistent with the provisions of this Article, shall continue in force until the General Assembly shall otherwise provide.

Section 4A. General laws for absentee voting.
The General Assembly shall enact general laws providing that any qualified elector of this State, duly registered, who shall be unable to appear to cast his or her ballot at any general election at the regular polling place of the election district in which he or she is registered, either because of being in the public service of the United States or of this State, or his or her spouse or dependents when residing with or accompanying him or her because of the nature of his or her business or occupation, because of his or her sickness or physical disability, because of his or her absence from the district while on vacation, or because of the tenets or teachings of his or her religion, may cast a ballot at such general election to be counted in such election district.

Section 4B. Uniform laws for absentee registration.
The General Assembly shall enact uniform laws for the registration of voters of this State entitled to vote under this Article who are temporarily absent therefrom and in the Armed Forces or Merchant Marine of the United States, or retainers or his or her spouse or dependents when residing with or accompanying him or her, or who are absent from the State because of illness or injury received while serving in any such capacity, upon application in person or in writing.

Section 5. Electors privileged from arrest; exceptions.
Electors shall in all cases, except treason, felony, or breach of the peace, be privileged from arrest, during their attendance at elections, and in going to and returning from them.

Section 6. Voting machine recording tapes, voting machine certificate, and absentee ballots; delivery to Prothonotary; duties and composition of court; quorum.
Said presiding election officer of each election district, following the close of the polls on the day of the general election, shall deliver the copy of each voting machine recording tape containing the signatures of the election officers present at the opening and closing of the polls from each voting machine assigned to his or her district and one copy of the voting machine certificate, made and certified by law, together with the ballot box or ballot boxes containing absentee ballots and other papers required by law to be placed therein, to the Prothonotary of the Superior Court of the county, who at 10 o'clock a.m. on the second day after the election present the same to the said Court, and the said Court shall at the same time convene for the performance of the duties hereby imposed upon it; and thereupon the said Court, with the aid of such of its officers and such sworn assistants as it shall appoint, shall publicly ascertain the state of the election throughout the county, by determining the aggregate number of votes for each office given in the election districts of the county and for every person who received votes for each office.

Said presiding election officer shall also deliver a copy of each voting machine recording tape from each voting machine assigned to his or her district, one copy of the voting machine certificate and absentee ballots to the Department of Elections following close of the polls on the day of the general election, which at 10 o'clock a.m. on the second day after the election and shall appear at said Court with said voting machine recording tapes, voting machine certificates and absentee ballots for use, as necessary, in ascertaining the state of the election.

In case any voting machine recording tape, voting machine certificate, absentee ballot box, and/or any other document required by law shall not be produced, or in the case of a complaint under oath of fraud or mistake in any such tape or certificate, or in case fraud or mistake is evident on the face of any document completed by any election officer, the Court shall have the power to issue summary process against any election officer or any other person to bring such persons forthwith into Court with the election papers in their possession or control; and to open any absentee ballot box and take therefrom any paper contained therein, and to recount the absentee ballots; and to correct any fraud or mistake on the voting machine recording tape(s) or on any document completed by any election officers relating to such election.

The said Court shall have all the other jurisdiction and powers now vested by law in the boards of canvass, and such other powers as shall be provided by law.
After the state of the election shall have been ascertained as aforesaid, the said Court shall make certificates thereof, under the seal of said Court in the form required by law, and transmit, deliver and lodge the same as required by this Constitution or by law, and deliver the ballot boxes to the sheriff of the county, to be by him or her kept and delivered as required by law.

No act or determination of the Court in the discharge of the duties imposed upon it by this section shall be conclusive in the trial of any contested election.

For the purposes of this section the Superior Court shall consist in New Castle County of the President Judge and resident Judge; in Kent County of the resident Judge and an Judge designated by the President Judge; and in Sussex County of the resident Judge and a Judge designated by the President Judge.

Two shall constitute a quorum. The Governor shall have power to commission a Judge for the purpose of constituting a quorum when by reason of legal exception to any Judge, or for any other cause, a quorum could not otherwise be had.

Section 7. Election offenses; penalties; self-incrimination. Every person who either in or out of the State shall receive or accept, or offer to receive or accept, or shall pay, transfer or deliver, or offer or promise to pay, transfer or deliver, or shall contribute, or offer or promise to contribute, to another to be paid or used, any money or other valuable thing as a compensation, inducement or reward for the giving or withholding, or in any manner influencing the giving or withholding, a vote at any general, special, or municipal election in this State, or at any primary election, convention or meeting held for the purpose of nominating any candidate or candidates to be voted for at such general, special or municipal election; or who either in or out of the State shall make or become directly or indirectly a party to any bet or wager depending upon the result of any such general, special, municipal or primary election or convention or meeting, or upon a vote thereat by any person; or who either in or out of the State shall, by the use or promise of money or other valuable thing, or otherwise, cause or attempt to cause any officer of election or registration officer to violate said person's official duty; or who either in or out of the State shall by the use or promise of money or other valuable thing influence or attempt to influence any person to be registered or abstain from being registered; or who, being an officer of election or registration officer, shall knowingly and wilfully violate said person's official duty; or who shall by force, threat, menace or intimidation, prevent or hinder, or attempt to prevent or hinder, any person qualified for registration from being registered or any person qualified to vote from voting according to said person's choice at any such general, special or municipal election, shall be deemed guilty of a misdemeanor, and shall be fined not less than one hundred dollars nor more than five thousand dollars, or shall be imprisoned for a term not less than one month nor more than three years, or shall suffer both fine and imprisonment within said limits, at the discretion of the court; and shall further for a term of ten years next following said person's sentence, be incapable of voting at any such general, special, municipal or primary election or convention or meeting; but the penalty of disfranchisement shall not apply to any person making or being a party to any bet or wager, depending upon the result of any such general, special, municipal or primary election or convention or meeting. Every person charged with the commission while out of the State of any of the offenses enumerated in this section, and by this section made punishable, whether committed in or out of the State, may be prosecuted under Section 8 of this Article in any county in which said person shall be arrested on such charge. No person, other than the accused, shall, in the prosecution for any offense mentioned in this section, be permitted to withhold said person's testimony on the ground that it may criminate said person or subject said person to public infamy; but such testimony shall not afterwards be used against said person in any judicial proceeding, except for perjury in giving such testimony.

Section 8. Prosecution for election offenses; procedure; appeal; bond.

Every prosecution for any of the offenses mentioned in Section 7 of this Article shall be on information filed by the Attorney-General, after examination and commitment or holding to bail by a judge or Justice of the Peace, and the cause shall be heard, tried and determined by the court without the intervention of either a grand jury or petit jury. The accused if adjudged guilty of the offense charged against him or her, shall have the right at any time within the space of three calendar months next after sentence is pronounced to an appeal to the Supreme Court. The court below, or any judge thereof, in term time or vacation, shall upon application by the accused allow such appeal; but such appeal shall not operate as a supersedeas unless the appellant shall at the time of the allowance thereof give an appeal bond to the State of Delaware in such amount and with such surety as shall be approved by such court or judge. On such appeal the Supreme Court shall, with all convenient speed, review the evidence adduced in the cause in the court below, as well as the other proceedings therein, and the law applicable thereto, and give final judgment accordingly, either affirming or reversing the judgment below. If the appellant shall fail to prosecute his or her appeal pursuant to the rules and practice hereinafter provided for, the Supreme Court shall affirm the judgment of the court below. Where the sentence in the court below includes a term of imprisonment and an appeal bond is given and approved in manner aforesaid, the Supreme Court, if it affirm the judgment below, shall sentence the appellant to a term of imprisonment equal to that imposed by the court below, after deducting therefrom a period equal to the time of imprisonment, if any, already suffered by him or her under the sentence of the court below. The surety or sureties in any appeal bond given under the provisions of this section shall have the right at any time after its approval and until final judgment shall be rendered by the Supreme Court, and, in case the judgment of the court below shall be affirmed, until the expiration of the space of thirty days next following such affirmance, to take, wherever found, and render the appellant to the sheriff of the county in which he or she was sentenced; and a certified copy of the appeal bond shall be the sufficient warrant for such surety or sureties for such taking and rendering. If the Supreme Court shall reverse any judgment of the court below imposing a fine, and if the accused shall have fully paid such fine and the costs of prosecution, the amount thereof shall be refunded to the appellant through a warrant drawn by the court below on the treasurer of the county in which the accused was sentenced. All the judges entitled to sit in the Supreme Court shall, as soon as conveniently may be, meet at the usual place of sitting of said court, and they, or a majority of them, shall adopt rules prescribing the forms and conditions of appeal bonds to be used under the provisions of this section, and the manner of certifying copies thereof, providing for the printing or reduction to writing of all oral evidence in the cause in the court below and of the opinion of said court, for the certification of the same when so printed or reduced to writing, and of copies thereof; for the copying and certification of all documentary or other written or printed evidence in the cause in the court below and of the record therein; for the transmission to the Supreme Court of such certified copies of such record, and of all the evidence adduced in the court below and of the opinion of said court for the transmission to the court below of a certified copy of the final judgment of the Supreme Court and of any additional sentence pronounced by said court, for the discharge of securities in appeal bonds, and for the framing, issuance, service and enforcement of all process and rules necessary to give full effect to the provisions of this section; and regulating generally the practice and procedure of the Supreme Court and the court below in cases of appeal under this section. The said judges, or a majority of them, met as aforesaid, may also provide that when complaint shall be made in due form, prescribed by them, to any judge entitled to sit in the Supreme Court, that any offense mentioned in Section 7 of this Article has been committed in the county in which such judge shall reside, or out of the State, such judge shall have power to cause the person charged with such offense to be arrested within any county of this State and brought before him or her, and to bind him or her with sufficient surety, or, for want of bail, commit him or her for his or her appearance and answer at the next term of the Court of General Sessions in such manner and under and pursuant to such rules and regulations as the said judges, or a majority of them, shall prescribe. From time to time hereafter, whenever a majority of all the judges entitled to sit in the Supreme Court shall so request, all of the judges so entitled shall, as soon as conveniently may be, meet at the usual place of sitting of said court; and they, or a majority of them, shall have power to revise, amend, add to or annul, any rule or rules theretofore adopted touching forms, practice or procedure in cases of appeal under this section, or arrest and binding or commitment for appearance and answer, in such manner and to such extent as in their judgment shall best serve to effectuate the purposes hereof. No person shall be adjudged guilty of an offense mentioned in Section 7 of this Article without the concurrence of all the judges trying the case; and upon appeal no judgment of the court below shall be affirmed without the concurrence of all of the judges of the Supreme Court sitting in the case, and their failure to concur as aforesaid shall operate as a reversal of the judgment of the court below; provided, however, that such concurrence of the judges sitting in the Supreme Court shall not be necessary for the affirmance of the judgment of the court below where the appellant shall fail to prosecute his or her appeal pursuant to the rules and practices herein provided for.

Section 9. Enumeration of election offenses as limitation on power of General Assembly.
The enumeration of the offenses mentioned in Section 7 of this Article shall not preclude the General Assembly from defining and providing for the punishment of other offenses against the freedom and purity of the ballot, or touching the conduct, returns or ascertainment of the result of general, special or municipal elections, or of primary elections, conventions or meetings held for the nomination of candidates to be voted for at general, special or municipal elections. No prosecution under any act of the General Assembly passed pursuant to this section shall be subject to the provisions of Section 8 of this Article.

ARTICLE VI: IMPEACHMENT AND TREASON

Section 1. Impeachment power of House; trial by Senate; oath of Senators; vote; presiding officers.

The House of Representatives shall have the sole power of impeaching; but two-thirds of all the members must concur in an impeachment. All impeachments shall be tried by the Senate, and when sitting for that purpose, the Senators shall be upon oath or affirmation to do justice according to the evidence. No person shall be convicted without the concurrence of two-thirds of all the Senators.

On the trial of an impeachment against the Governor or Lieutenant-Governor, the Chief Justice, or, in case of his or her absence or disability, the Chancellor shall preside; and on the trial of all other impeachments the President of the Senate shall preside.

Section 2. Grounds for impeachment.

The Governor and all other civil officers under this State shall be liable to impeachment for treason, bribery, or any high crime or misdemeanor in office. Judgment in such cases shall not extend further than to removal from office, and disqualification to hold any office of honor, trust or profit, under this State; but the party convicted shall, nevertheless, be subject to indictment, trial, judgment and punishment according to law.

Section 3. Treason.

Treason against this State shall consist only in levying war against it, or in adhering to the enemies of the Government, giving them aid and comfort. No person shall be convicted of treason unless on the testimony of two witnesses to the same overt act or on confession in open court.

ARTICLE VII: PARDONS

Section 1. Power of Governor; recommendation of Board of Pardons; entry in register and submission to General Assembly.

The Governor shall have power to remit fines and forfeitures and to grant reprieves, commutations of sentence and pardons, except in cases of impeachment; but no pardon, or reprieve for more than six months, shall be granted, nor sentence commuted, except upon the recommendation in writing of a majority of the Board of Pardons after full hearing; and such recommendation, with the reasons therefor at length, shall be filed and recorded in the office of the Secretary of State, who shall forthwith notify the Governor thereof.

He or she shall fully set forth in writing the grounds of all reprieves, pardons and remissions, to be entered in the register of his or her official acts and laid before the General Assembly at its next session.

Section 2. Composition of Board of Pardons.

The Board of Pardons shall be composed of the Chancellor, Lieutenant-Governor, Secretary of State, State Treasurer and Auditor of Accounts.

Section 3. Information from Attorney General on Board's duties.

The said board may require information from the Attorney-General upon any subject relating to the duties of said board.

ARTICLE VIII: REVENUE AND TAXATION

Section 1. Uniformity of taxes; collection under general laws; exemption for public welfare purposes.

All taxes shall be uniform upon the same class of subjects within the territorial limits of the authority levying the tax, except as otherwise permitted herein, and shall be levied and collected under general laws passed by the General Assembly. County Councils of New Castle and Sussex Counties and the Levy Court of Kent County are hereby authorized to exempt from county taxation such property in their respective counties as in their opinion will best promote the public welfare. The county property tax exemption power created by this section shall be exclusive as to such property as is located within the respective counties. With respect to real property located within the boundaries of any incorporated municipality, the authority to exempt such property from municipal property tax shall be exercised by the respective incorporated municipality, when in the opinion of said municipality it will best promote the public welfare.

The legislature shall enact laws to provide that the value of land which is determined by the assessing officer of the taxing jurisdiction to be actively devoted to agriculture use and to have been so devoted for at least the two successive years immediately preceding the tax year in issue, shall, for local tax purposes, on application of the owner, be that value which such land has for agricultural use.

Any such laws shall provide that when land which has been valued in this manner for local tax purposes is applied to a use other than for agriculture, it shall be subject to additional taxes in an amount equal to the difference, if any, between the taxes paid or payable on the basis of the valuation and the assessment authorized hereunder and the taxes that would have been paid or payable had the land been valued and assessed as otherwise provided in this Constitution, in the current year and in such of the tax years immediately preceding, not less than two such years in which the land was valued as herein authorized.

Such laws shall also provide for the assessment and collection of any additional taxes levied thereupon and shall include such other provisions as shall be necessary to carry out the provisions of this amendment.

Section 2. Revenue bills to originate in House; amendments by Senate; restriction on definition; exclusion of unrelated matter.

All bills for raising revenue shall originate in the House of Representatives; but the Senate may propose alterations as on other bills; and no bill from the operation of which, when passed into a law, revenue may incidentally arise shall be accounted a bill for raising revenue; nor shall any matter or cause whatever not immediately relating to and necessary for raising revenue be in any manner blended with or annexed to a bill for raising revenue.

Section 3. Borrowing money; specification of purpose; surplus borrowed money.

No money shall be borrowed or debt created by or on behalf of the State but pursuant to an Act of the General Assembly, passed with the concurrence of three fourths of all the members elected to each House, except to supply casual deficiencies of revenue, repel invasion, suppress insurrection, defend the State in war, or pay existing debts; and any law authorizing the borrowing of money by or on behalf of the State shall specify the purpose for which the money is to be borrowed, and the money so borrowed shall be used exclusively for such purpose; but should the money so borrowed or any part thereof be left after the abandonment of such purpose or the accomplishment thereof, such money, or the surplus thereof, may be disposed of according to law.

Section 4. Restrictions on loan of public money or bonds and credit of State.

No appropriation of the public money shall be made to, nor the bonds of this State be issued or loaned to any county, municipality or corporation, nor shall the credit of the State, by the guarantee or the endorsement of the bonds or other undertakings of any county, municipality or corporation, be pledged otherwise than pursuant to an Act of the General Assembly, passed with the concurrence of three fourths of all the members elected to each House.

Section 5. Capitation tax; uniformity; use.

The General Assembly shall provide for levying and collecting a capitation tax from every citizen of the State of the age of twenty-one years or upwards; but such tax to be collected in any County shall be uniform throughout that County, and such capitation tax shall be used exclusively in the County in which it is collected.

Section 6. Procedure in withdrawal and payment of public moneys; annual publication of receipts and expenditures; limitation upon appropriations.

(a) No money shall be drawn from the treasury but pursuant to an appropriation made by Act of the General Assembly; provided, however, that the compensation of the members of the General Assembly and all expenses connected with the session thereof may be paid out of the treasury pursuant to resolution in that behalf; a regular account of the receipts and expenditures of all public money shall be published annually.

(b) No appropriation, supplemental appropriation or budget act shall cause the aggregate State General Fund appropriations enacted for any given fiscal year to exceed 98 percent of the estimated State General Fund revenue for such fiscal year from all sources, including estimated unencumbered funds remaining at the end of the previous fiscal year. An act approved pursuant to Section 3 of this article shall not be considered an appropriation for the purpose of this section. Estimated unencumbered funds are calculated by taking the estimated General Fund cash balance at the end of the fiscal year less estimated revenue anticipation bonds or notes, estimated encumbrances, estimated continuing appropriations and the amount of the Budget Reserve Account as established in subsection (d) of this section at the end of said fiscal year. The amount of said revenue estimate and estimated unencumbered funds remaining shall be determined by the most recent joint resolution approved from time to time by a majority of the members elected to each House of the General Assembly and signed by the Governor.

(c) Notwithstanding subsection (b) of this section, any portion of the amount between 98 and 100 percent of the estimated State General Fund revenue for any fiscal year as estimated in accordance with subsection (b) of this section may be appropriated in any given fiscal year in the event of emergencies involving the health, safety or welfare of the citizens of the State, such appropriations to be approved by three-fifths of the members elected to each House of the General Assembly.

(d) There is hereby established a Budget Reserve Account within the General Fund. Within 45 days after the end of any fiscal year, the excess of any unencumbered funds remaining from the said fiscal year shall be paid into the Budget Reserve Account, provided, however, that no such payment will be made which would increase the total of the Budget Reserve Account to more than 5 percent of only the estimated State General Fund revenues as set by subsection (b) of this section. The excess of any unencumbered funds shall be determined by subtracting from the actual unencumbered funds at the end of any fiscal year an amount which together with the latest estimated revenues is necessary to fund the ensuing fiscal year's General Fund budget including the required estimated General Fund supplemental and automatic appropriations for said ensuing fiscal year less estimated reversions. The General Assembly by a three-fifths vote of the members elected to each House, may appropriate from the Budget Reserve Account such additional sums as may be necessary to fund any unanticipated deficit in any given fiscal year or to provide funds required as a result of any revenue reduction enacted by the General Assembly.

Section 7. Real estate assessments; inclusion of values.
In all assessments of the value of real estate for taxation, the value of the land and the value of the buildings and improvements thereon shall be included. And in all assessments of the rental value of real estate for taxation, the rental value of the land and the rental value of the buildings and the improvements thereon shall be included. The foregoing provisions of this section shall apply to all assessments of the value of real estate or of the rental value thereof for taxation for State, county, hundred, school, municipal or other public purposes.

Section 8. Lending credit, appropriating money to or becoming interested in any private corporation, person or company by county or municipality.
No county, city, town or other municipality shall lend its credit or appropriate money to, or assume the debt of, or become a shareholder or joint owner in or with any private corporation or any person or company whatever.

Section 9. Retroactive increase of taxation of personal income.
Any law which shall have the effect of increasing the rates of taxation on personal income for any year or part thereof prior to the date of the enactment thereof, or for any year or years prior to the year in which the law is enacted, shall be void.

Section 10. Limitation on increase of rate of taxes and license fees; exception to meet obligation under faith and credit pledge; allocation of public moneys to meet such obligation if revenues are not sufficient to meet such pledge.

(a) The effective rate of any tax levied or license fee imposed by the State may not be increased except pursuant to an act of the General Assembly adopted with the concurrence of three-fifths of all members of each House.

(b) Prior to the beginning of each fiscal year of the State, the General Assembly shall appropriate revenues of the State to pay interest on its debt to which it has pledged its faith and credit and which interest is payable in the year for which such appropriation is made and to pay the principal of such debt, payable in such year, whether at maturity or otherwise. To the extent that insufficient revenues of the State are available to pay principal of and interest on such debt when due and payable, the first public moneys of the State thereafter received shall be set aside and applied to the payment of the principal of and interest on such debt. To make up for such insufficient revenues, the General Assembly may increase the rate of taxes and fees without regard to the limitations of subsection (a) hereof after the failure to pay when due the principal of and interest on such debt.

Section 11. Imposition or levy of new taxes or license fees.

(a) No tax or license fee may be imposed or levied except pursuant to an act of the General Assembly adopted with the concurrence of three-fifths of all members of each House.
(b) Prior to the beginning of each fiscal year of the State, the General Assembly shall appropriate revenues of the State to pay interest on its debt to which it has pledged its faith and credit and which interest is payable in the year for which such appropriation is made and to pay the principal of such debt, payable in such year, whether at maturity or otherwise. To the extent that insufficient revenues of the State are available to pay principal of and interest on such debt when due and payable, the first public moneys of the State thereafter received shall be set aside and applied to the payment of the principal of and interest on such debt. To make up for such insufficient revenues, the General Assembly may increase the rate of taxes and fees without regard to the limitations of subsection (a) hereof after the failure to pay when due the principal of and interest on such debt.

(c) This amendment shall not apply to any tax or license fee authorized by an act of the General Assembly but not effective upon the effective date of this amendment.

Section 12. The Transportation Trust Fund; use and restrictions.

(a) The State irrevocably pledges and assigns and continuously appropriates the proceeds derived from a motor vehicle registration fee, a motor vehicle document fee, a motor fuel tax, a motor carrier road use tax and registration fee, and the operation of the Delaware Turnpike to a special fund known as the Transportation Trust Fund.

(b) The moneys in the Transportation Trust Fund may be appropriated and used for the following purposes:

(1) Capital expenditures on the public transportation system, including the road system, grants and allocations for investments in transportation, the transit system, and the support systems for public transportation.

(2) Payment of the interest and principal on all indebtedness incurred before or after the effective date of this Act, including the payment of all other obligations incurred pursuant to any trust agreement related to such indebtedness, and secured by moneys in the Transportation Trust Fund.

(3) Other transportation-related purposes, including operating expenses, to which moneys in the Transportation Trust Fund are authorized on the effective date of this Act.

(c) No moneys in the Transportation Trust Fund may be appropriated for a purpose not listed in subsection (b) of this section except by an act of the General Assembly adopted with the concurrence of three-fourths of all members of each House and separate from an annual budget act, bond and capital improvement act, or grants-in-aid act.

(d) If moneys in the Transportation Trust Fund cease to be appropriated for a purpose under paragraph (b)(3) of this section, the moneys may not again be appropriated for a purpose under paragraph (b)(3) of this section except by an act of the General Assembly adopted with the concurrence of three-fourths of all members of each House and separate from an annual budget act, bond and capital improvement act, or grants-in-aid act.

ARTICLE IX: CORPORATIONS

Section 1. Creation, amendment, renewal or revival by general law; exceptions; revocation or forfeitures of charters; requisites for enactment of corporation laws.

No corporation shall hereafter be created, amended, renewed or revived by special act, but only by or under general law, nor shall any existing corporate charter be amended, renewed or revived by special act, but only by or under general law; but the foregoing provisions shall not apply to municipal corporations, banks or corporations for charitable, penal, reformatory, or educational purposes, sustained in whole or in part by the State.

The General Assembly shall, by general law, provide for the revocation or forfeiture of the charters of all corporations for the abuse, misuse, or non-user of their corporate powers, privileges or franchises. Any proceeding for such revocation or forfeiture, shall be taken by the Attorney-General, as may be provided by law. No general incorporation law, nor any special act of incorporation, shall be enacted without the concurrence of two-thirds of all the members elected to each House of the General Assembly.

Section 2. Acceptance of Constitution by existing corporations as prerequisite for amendment or renewal of charter.

No corporation in existence at the adoption of this Constitution shall have its charter amended or renewed without first filing, under the corporate seal of said corporation, and duly attested, in the office of the Secretary of State, an acceptance of the provisions of this Constitution.

Section 3. Issuance of stock.

Repealed.

Section 4. Rights, privileges, immunities and estates.

The rights, privileges, immunities and estates of religious societies and corporate bodies, except as herein otherwise provided, shall remain as if the Constitution of this State had not been altered.

Section 5. Designation, by foreign corporation, of agent for service of process.

No foreign corporation shall do any business in this State through or by branch offices, agents or representatives located in this State, without having an authorized agent or agents in the State upon whom legal process may be served.

Section 6. Taxation of stock owned by persons or corporations without the State.

Shares of the capital stock of corporations created under the laws of this State, when owned by persons or corporations without this State, shall not be subject to taxation by any law now existing or hereafter to be made.

ARTICLE X: EDUCATION

Section 1. Establishment and maintenance of free public schools; attendance.

The General Assembly shall provide for the establishment and maintenance of a general and efficient system of free public schools, and may require by law that every child, not physically or mentally disabled, shall attend the public school, unless educated by other means.

Section 2. Annual appropriations; apportionment; use of funds; separation of schools; other expenses.

In addition to the income of the investments of the Public School Fund, the General Assembly shall make provision for the annual payment of not less than one hundred thousand dollars for the benefit of the free public schools which, with the income of the investments of the Public School Fund, shall be equitably apportioned among the school districts of the State as the General Assembly shall provide; and the money so apportioned shall be used exclusively for the payment of teachers' salaries and for furnishing free text books; provided, however, that in such apportionment, no distinction shall be made on account of race or color. All other expenses connected with the maintenance of free public schools, and all expenses connected with the erection or repair of free public school buildings shall be defrayed in such manner as shall be provided by law.

Section 3. Use of educational funds by religious schools; exemption of school property from taxation.

No portion of any fund now existing, or which may hereafter be appropriated, or raised by tax, for educational purposes, shall be appropriated to, or used by, or in aid of any sectarian, church or denominational school; provided, that all real or personal property used for school purposes, where the tuition is free, shall be exempt from taxation and assessment for public purposes.

Section 4. Use of Public School Fund.

No part of the principal or income of the Public School Fund, now or hereafter existing, shall be used for any other purpose than the support of free public schools.

Section 5. Transportation of nonpublic school students.

The General Assembly, notwithstanding any other provision of this Constitution, may provide by an Act of the General Assembly, passed with the concurrence of a majority of all the members elected to each House, for the transportation of students of nonpublic, nonprofit Elementary and High Schools.

Section 6. Property tax; use limitations.

No property tax receipts received by a public school district as a result of a property tax levied for a particular purpose shall be used for any other purpose except upon the favorable vote of a majority of the eligible voters in the district voting on the question.

ARTICLE XI: AGRICULTURE

Section 1. State Board of Agriculture.
There shall be a department established and maintained, known as the State Board of Agriculture.

Section 2. Composition of Board; residence of Commissioners; quorum.
The said board shall be composed of three Commissioners of Agriculture, one of whom shall reside in each county in the State. Any two of them shall constitute a quorum for the transaction of business.

Section 3. Appointment of Commissioners by Governor; tenure; vacancies.
The said Commissioners of Agriculture shall be appointed by the Governor, by and with the consent of a majority of all the members elected to the Senate, one for the term of one year, one for the term of two years, and one for the term of three years; and thereafter all appointments of Commissioners of Agriculture shall be made as aforesaid for the term of three years, and they shall hold office until their successors are duly qualified; provided, that any vacancy occurring in the office of Commissioner of Agriculture before the expiration of a term shall be filled by appointment as aforesaid for the remainder of the term; and provided further, that in case such vacancy shall occur when the Senate is not in session, such vacancy may be filled by the Governor without confirmation by the Senate until the end of the next session of the Senate.

Section 4. Abatement and prevention of diseases of fruit trees, plants, vegetables, cereals and livestock.
The said board shall have power to abate and prevent, by such means as the General Assembly shall prescribe, all contagious and infectious diseases of fruit trees, plants, vegetables, cereals, horses, cattle and other farm animals.

Section 5. Plans for securing immigration of industrious and useful settlers.

The said Commissioners may devise such plans for securing immigration to this State of industrious and useful settlers as they may deem expedient, and such plans may be executed as prescribed by the General Assembly.

Section 6. Compensation of Board members.

The General Assembly shall provide by law for the compensation of the members of said board.

Section 7. Duration of Board.

The Board of Agriculture hereby established shall continue for eight years from the date of the qualification of the first member thereof, after which it may be abolished by the General Assembly.

ARTICLE XII

Section 1. State Board of Health; local boards; powers.

Repealed.

ARTICLE XIII: LOCAL OPTION

Section 1. Submission of liquor question to district electors; election.

The General Assembly may from time to time provide by law for the submission to the vote of the qualified electors of the several districts of the State, or any of them, mentioned in Section 2 of this Article, the question whether the manufacture and sale of intoxicating liquors shall be licensed or prohibited within the limits thereof; and in every district in which there is a majority against license, no person, firm or corporation shall thereafter manufacture or sell spirituous, vinous or malt liquors, except for medicinal or sacramental purposes, within said district, until at a subsequent submission of such question a majority of votes shall be cast in said district for license. Whenever a majority of all the members elected to each House of the General Assembly by the qualified electors in any district named in Section 2 of this Article shall request the submission of the question of license or no license to a vote of the qualified electors in said district, the General Assembly shall provide for the submission of such question to the qualified electors in such district at the next general election thereafter.

Section 2. Designation of districts for purposes of article.

Under the provisions of this Article, Sussex County shall comprise one district, Kent County one district, the City of Wilmington, as its corporate limits now are or may hereafter be extended, one district, and the remaining part of New Castle County one district.

Section 3. Laws for enforcement, manufacture and sale, and penalties.

The General Assembly shall provide necessary laws to carry out and enforce the provisions of this Article, enact laws governing the manufacture and sale of intoxicating liquors under the limitation of this Article, and provide such penalties as may be necessary to enforce the same.

ARTICLE XIV: OATH OF OFFICE

Section 1. Form of oath for members of General Assembly and public officers.

Members of the General Assembly and all public officers executive and judicial, except such inferior officers as shall be by law exempted, shall, before they enter upon the duties of their respective offices, take and subscribe the following oath or affirmation:

"I, (name) , do proudly swear (or affirm) to carry out the responsibilities of the office of
(name of office) to the best of my ability, freely acknowledging that the powers of this office flow from the people I am privileged to represent. I further swear (or affirm) always to place the public interests above any special or personal interests, and to respect the right of future generations to share the rich historic and natural heritage of Delaware. In doing so I will always uphold and defend the Constitutions of my Country and my State, so help me God."

No other oath, declaration or test shall be required as a qualification for any office of public trust.

ARTICLE XV: MISCELLANEOUS

Section 1. Conservators of the peace.
The Chancellor, Judges and Attorney-General shall be conservators of the peace throughout the State; and the Sheriffs shall be conservators of the peace within the counties respectively in which they reside.

Section 2. Receipt for fees.
No public officer shall receive any fees without giving to the person paying the same a receipt therefor, if required, therein specifying every item and charge.

Section 3. Costs on bill returned ignoramus or on acquittal.
No costs shall be paid by a person accused, on a bill returned ignoramus, nor on acquittal.

Section 4. Extension of term of public officer; diminution of salary or emoluments.
No law shall extend the term of any public officer or diminish the salary or emoluments after his or her election or appointment. The term "salary or emoluments" as used herein refers to the actual salary or emoluments being provided an officer at any time during his or her tenure in office and shall not be construed to mean increases in salary or emoluments scheduled by statute for a future date and not yet received by the officer.

Section 5. Officers to hold office until successors qualify.
All public officers shall hold their respective offices until their successors shall be duly qualified, except in cases herein otherwise provided.

Section 6. Behavior of officers; removal for misbehavior or infamous crime.
All public officers shall hold their offices on condition that they behave themselves well. The Governor shall remove from office any public officer convicted of misbehavior in office or of any

infamous crime.

Section 7. Offenses excepted from prohibition against prosecuting by information and jury trial.
The matters within Section 30 of Article IV and Sections 7 and 8 of Article V are excepted from the provision of the Constitution that "No person shall for any indictable offense be proceeded against criminally by information," and also from the provisions of the Constitution concerning trial by jury.

Section 8. Interest of member or officer of department in contracts for supplies or services of department prohibited.
No member or officer of any department of the government shall be in any way interested in any contract for the furnishing of stationery, printing, paper and fuel used in the legislative and other departments of government; or for the printing, binding and distributing of the laws, journals, official reports, and all other printing and binding, and the repairing and furnishing the halls and rooms used for the meetings of the General Assembly and its committees, when such contract is awarded to or by any such member, officer or department.

Section 9. Prefixing Constitution to codification of laws.
This Constitution shall be prefixed to every codification of the Laws of this State.

Section 10. Disqualification to hold office by reason of sex.
No citizen of the State of Delaware shall be disqualified to hold and enjoy any office, or public trust, under the laws of this State, by reason of sex.

ARTICLE XVI: AMENDMENTS AND CONVENTIONS

Section 1. Proposal of Constitutional amendments in General Assembly; procedure.

Any amendment or amendments to this Constitution may be proposed in the Senate or House of Representatives; and if the same shall be agreed to by two thirds of all the members elected to each House, such proposed amendment or amendments shall be entered on their journals, with the yeas and nays taken thereon, and the Secretary of State shall cause such proposed amendment or amendments to be published three months before the next general election in at least three newspapers in each county in which such newspapers shall be published; and if in the General Assembly next after the said election such proposed amendment or amendments shall upon yea and nay vote be agreed to by two thirds of all the members elected to each House, the same shall thereupon become part of the Constitution.

Section 2. Constitutional Conventions; procedure; compensation of delegates; quorum; powers and duties; vacancies.

The General Assembly by a two-thirds vote of all the members elected to each House may from time to time provide for the submission to the qualified electors of the State at the general election next thereafter the question, "Shall there be a Convention to revise the Constitution and amend the same"; and upon such submission, if a majority of those voting on said question shall decide in favor of a Convention for such purpose, the General Assembly at its next session shall provide for the election of delegates to such Convention at the next general election. Such Convention shall be composed of forty-one delegates, one of whom shall be chosen from each Representative District by the qualified electors thereof, and two of whom shall be chosen from New Castle County, two from Kent County and two from Sussex County by the qualified electors thereof respectively. The delegates so chosen shall convene at the Capital of the State on the first Tuesday in September next after their election. Every delegate shall receive for his or her services such compensation as shall be provided by law. A majority of the Convention shall constitute a quorum for the transaction of business. The Convention shall have power to appoint such officers, employers and assistants as it may deem necessary, and fix their compensation, and provide for the printing of its documents, journals, debates and proceedings. The Convention shall determine the rules of its proceedings, and be the judge of the elections, returns and qualification of its members. Whenever there shall be a vacancy in the office of delegate from any district or county by reason of failure to elect, ineligibility, death, resignation or otherwise, a writ of election to fill such vacancy shall be issued by the Governor, and such vacancy shall be filled by the qualified electors of such district or county.

Section 3. Receiving, tallying and counting votes for or against Convention; return of vote; enabling legislation.
The General Assembly shall provide for receiving, tallying and counting the votes for or against a Convention, and for returning to the General Assembly at its next session the state of such vote; and shall also enact all provisions necessary for giving effect to this Article.

Section 4. Approval of bills or resolutions under this article; exemption from Article III, section 18.
No bill or resolution passed by the General Assembly under or pursuant to the provisions of this Article, shall require for its validity the approval of the Governor, and the same shall be exempt from the provisions of Section 18 of Article III, of this Constitution.

Section 5. Separate ballots on question of Convention.
In voting at any general election, upon the question, "Shall there be a Convention to revise the Constitution and amend the same?", the ballots shall be separate from those cast for any person voted for at such election, and shall be kept distinct and apart from all other ballots.

ARTICLE XVII: CONTINUITY OF GOVERNMENTAL OPERATIONS

Section 1. Continuity of state and local governmental operations in periods of emergency resulting from disasters caused by enemy attack.

The General Assembly, in order to insure continuity of State and local governmental operations in periods of emergency resulting from disasters caused by enemy attack, shall have the power and the immediate duty (1) to provide for prompt and temporary succession to the powers and duties of public offices whose succession is not otherwise provided for in this Constitution, of whatever nature and whether filled by election or appointment, the incumbents of which may become unavailable for carrying on the powers and duties of such offices, and (2) to adopt such other measures as may be necessary and proper for insuring the continuity of governmental operations. In the exercise of the powers hereby conferred the General Assembly shall in all respects conform to the requirements of this Constitution except to the extent that in the judgment of the General Assembly so to do would be impracticable or would admit of undue delay.

SCHEDULE

Section 1. Delivery, filing and publication of enrolled copy of amended Constitution and Schedule.

The President of this Convention, immediately on its adjournment, shall deliver the enrolled copy of this amended Constitution and Schedule to the Secretary of State, who shall file the same in his or her office, and the Secretary of this Convention shall cause the same to be published three times in two newspapers in each county of the State.

Section 2. Effective date of amended Constitution.

This amended Constitution shall take effect on the tenth day of June in the year one thousand eight hundred and ninety-seven.

Section 3. Effect on offices of Senators and Representatives; election.

The offices of the present Senators and Representatives shall not be vacated or otherwise affected by this amended Constitution, except that the Senators whose terms do not expire on the day of the next general election shall thereafter represent the districts in which they now reside until the end of the terms for which they were elected.

At the general election to be held in the year one thousand eight hundred and ninety-eight, there shall be elected from each of the even numbered Senatorial Districts in the State, except District number two in New Castle County, District number four in Kent County, and District number two in Sussex County, a Senator for the term of two years, and from each of the odd numbered Senatorial Districts in the State a Senator for the term of four years.

And thereafter, as the said terms shall from time to time expire, a Senator shall be elected from each of the said Senatorial Districts for the full term of four years.

At the general election to be held in the year one thousand eight hundred and ninety-eight, there shall be elected in each Representative District in the State one Representative for the term of two years.

Section 4. Commencement of terms of members of General Assembly.
The terms of Senators and Representatives shall begin on the day next after their election.

Section 5. Date of first general election.
The first general election under this amended Constitution shall be held on the Tuesday next after the first Monday in the month of November in the year one thousand eight hundred and ninety-eight.

Section 6. Effect on Governor's term.
The term of office of the present Governor shall not be vacated, or in any wise affected by this amended Constitution.

Section 7. Continuation of elective and appointive offices; election of successors; renewal of official obligations.
Unless otherwise provided by this amended Constitution or Schedule, all persons elected or appointed before this amended Constitution shall take effect, to State or county offices made elective by this amended Constitution, whose terms will expire before the first Tuesday in January in the year one thousand eight hundred and ninety-nine, shall hold their respective offices until the said last mentioned day; and all persons elected or appointed as aforesaid to such offices, whose terms will expire between the said first Tuesday in January in the year one thousand eight hundred and ninety-nine and the first Tuesday in January in the year one thousand nine hundred and one, shall hold their respective offices until the said last mentioned day; and all persons elected or appointed as aforesaid to such offices, whose terms will expire between the said first Tuesday in January in the year one thousand nine hundred and one and the

first Tuesday in January in the year one thousand nine hundred and three, shall hold their respective offices until the said last mentioned day; and the successors of such persons shall be elected at the general election next before the expiration of the terms as hereby extended; provided, however, that the successors of the present Auditor of Accounts, State Treasurer and Insurance Commissioner shall be elected at the general election next preceding the expiration of their several terms of office, and the persons so elected shall enter upon the duties of their respective offices on the first Tuesday in January following their election. The officers whose terms of office are extended by this section shall renew their official obligations upon the expiration of their present terms.

Section 8. Date of commencement of terms of elective officers.

The terms of office of all State and County officers made elective by this amended Constitution shall commence on the first Tuesday in January next after their election, unless otherwise provided in this amended Constitution or Schedule.

Section 9. Date of abolition of courts and judicial offices; transfer of pending proceedings and books, records and papers.

All the courts of justice now existing shall continue with their present jurisdiction, and the Chancellor and judges shall continue in office until the tenth day of June in the year one thousand eight hundred and ninety-seven; upon which day the said courts shall be abolished, and the offices of the said Chancellor and judges shall expire.

All writs of error, and appeals and proceedings which, on the said tenth day of June in the year one thousand eight hundred and ninety-seven shall be depending in the Court of Errors and Appeals, and all the books, records and papers of said court, shall be transferred to the Supreme Court established by this amended Constitution; and the said writs of error, appeals and proceedings shall be proceeded in the said Supreme Court to final judgment, decree or other determination.

All suits, proceedings, and matters which, on the said tenth day of June in the year one thousand eight hundred and ninety-seven, shall be depending in the Superior Court, and all books, records and papers of the said court, shall be transferred to the Superior Court established by this amended Constitution, and the said suits, proceedings and matters shall be proceeded in to final judgment, or determination, in the said Superior Court established by this amended Constitution.

All indictments, proceedings and matters which, on the said tenth day of June in the year one thousand eight hundred and ninety-seven, shall be depending in the Court of General Sessions of the Peace and Jail Delivery shall be transferred to and proceeded in to final judgment and determination in the Court of General Sessions established by this amended Constitution, or be otherwise disposed of by the Court of General Sessions, and all books, records and papers of said Court of General Sessions of the Peace and Jail Delivery shall be transferred to the said Court of General Sessions.

All indictments, proceedings and matters which, on the said tenth day of June in the year one thousand eight hundred and ninety-seven, shall be depending in the Court of Oyer and Terminer, shall be transferred to and proceeded in to final judgment and determination in the Court of Oyer and Terminer, established by this amended Constitution, and all books, records and papers of said Court of Oyer and Terminer shall be transferred to said Court of Oyer and Terminer established by this amended Constitution.

All suits, proceedings and matters which, on the said tenth day of June in the year one thousand eight hundred and ninety-seven, shall be depending in the Court of Chancery, or in the Orphans' Court, and all records, books and papers of said courts respectively, shall be transferred to Court of Chancery or Orphans' Court respectively, established by this amended

Constitution; and the suits, proceedings and matters, shall be proceeded in to final decree, order or other determination.

Section 10. Registers' Court and jurisdiction of justice of the peace unaffected.
Unless otherwise provided, the Registers' Courts and the jurisdiction of Justice of the Peace shall not be affected by this amended Constitution.

Section 11. Payments to certain incumbent judges not reappointed.
If the Chancellor, Chief Justice or any Judge in office at the time this amended Constitution shall take effect shall not be appointed Chancellor, Chief Justice or Judge under this amended Constitution, he or she shall be entitled to receive the sum of fifteen hundred dollars per annum, payable quarterly, for five years, after the expiration of his or her office, if he or she shall so long live.

Section 12. First biennial session of General Assembly under Constitution.
The first biennial session of the General Assembly under this amended Constitution shall commence on the first Tuesday in January in the year one thousand eight hundred and ninety-nine.

Section 13. Exceptions to limitations on amount of compensation payable to members of General Assembly and presiding officers.
The provisions of Section 15 of Article II of this amended Constitution limiting the amount of the compensation of the members of the General Assembly and the presiding officers of the respective Houses shall not apply to any adjourned, special or extra session of the General Assembly held prior to the first Tuesday in January in the year one thousand eight hundred and ninety-nine.

Section 14. Renewal of existing corporations until enactment of general incorporation law.

Until the General Assembly shall enact a general incorporation law as provided for in Section 1 of Article IX of this amended Constitution, existing corporations may, be renewed for a period not exceeding four years, without change or enlargement of their corporate powers or duties, in the manner lawful before this amended Constitution shall take effect.

Section 15. Guardians' accounts.

Until the General Assembly shall otherwise provide, guardians' accounts shall be filed with and be adjusted and settled by the Register of Wills for the county, and be subject to exception, hearing, adjustment and settlement in the Orphans' Court for the county as before this amended Constitution took effect.

Section 16. Terms of office of persons holding office on effective date of Constitution.

Unless otherwise provided by this amended Constitution or Schedule, the terms of persons holding public offices to which they have been elected or appointed at the time this amended Constitution and Schedule shall take effect, shall not be vacated or otherwise affected thereby.

Section 17. Vacancies in Board of Pardons.

One or more vacancies in the Board of Pardons shall not invalidate any act of the remaining members of said Board not less than three in number.

Section 18. Laws consistent with Constitution not affected.

All the laws of this State existing at the time this Constitution shall take effect, and not inconsistent with it shall remain in force, except so far as they shall be altered by future laws.

Section 19. Enabling legislation.
The General Assembly, as soon as conveniently may be after this Constitution shall take effect, shall enact all laws necessary or proper for carrying out the provisions thereof.

DONE IN CONVENTION, the fourth day of June in the year of our Lord one thousand eight hundred and ninety-seven and of the Independence of the United States of America the one hundred and twenty-first.

IN TESTIMONY WHEREOF , we have hereunto subscribed our names.

John Biggs, President.

Edward G. Bradford,
Charles B. Evans,
George H. Murray,
Martin B. Burris,
James B. Gilchrist,
William P. Orr,
Jr., William A. Cannon,
Robert G. Harman,
Nathan Pratt,
Paris T. Carlisle,
Jr., Edward D. Hearne,
Charles F. Richards,
Wilson T. Cavender,
Andrew J. Horsey,
Lowder L. Sapp,
David S. Clark,
John W. Hering,
William Saulsbury,
J. Wilkins Cooch,
Andrew L. Johnson,
William T. Smithers,
Ezekiel W. Cooper,
Woodburn Martin,

W. C. Spruance,
Robert W. Dasey,
Elias N. Moore,
Isaac K. Wright,
Joshua A. Ellegood.

Attest: Charles R. Jones, Secretary of C.C.

www.ingramcontent.com/pod-product-compliance
Lightning Source LLC
Chambersburg PA
CBHW070145230526
45471CB00002B/525